T0198863

MINING
FOR
MASTERPIECES

DIGGING FOR ANOTHER DIMENSION

DR. AARON CHAPMAN

authorHOUSE®

AuthorHouse™
1663 Liberty Drive
Bloomington, IN 47403
www.authorhouse.com
Phone: 1 (800) 839-8640

Published by AuthorHouse 05/14/2018

ISBN: 978-1-5462-4106-5 (sc)
ISBN: 978-1-5462-4105-8 (e)

New American Standard Bible (NASB)
Copyright © 1960, 1962, 1963, 1968, 1971, 1972, 1973,
1975, 1977, 1995 by The Lockman Foundation

Contents

Preface

This Homiletic text was birthed from my burning desire to witness clergy maximizing their potential. In the Ecclesiastical Sector, there are many preachers deprived of a fighting chance in ministry. Unfortunately, several clergy leaders lack the patience, time and/or ability to articulate the process of preaching in an understandable and relevant approach without demeaning the preacher for what they don't know.

Mining for Masterpieces encourages you to take digging to another dimension and is a textual follow up to my previous literary preaching text, I'm Called to Preach: Now What? This text "Mining for Masterpieces" is formatted in such a way that the layman, the academician, the scholar and/or the untrained clergy may develop an ear and a passion for preaching as they're engaging in healthy practices that will yield homiletic improvement over time.

In this era of postmodernity, I believe that the simple tenants of the faith are being tauntingly tortured and tantalized daily. There are sinners and saints who believe that preaching is the terrorist to societal enjoyment. This is why they are found saying in regular dialogical exchange "don't preach to me!" Mind you, it doesn't even have to be a religious conversation! Preaching has been degraded in some churches down to sawdust! Even some seminary curriculums are congested with Church Administrative electives while neglecting one of the central activities of the pastorate, which is honing the homiletic craft (preaching).

It is my desire to create a gold rush, an irrepressible fever that will ignite the passion for godly knowledge and for preaching with passion the good news of Jesus Christ. It is important that we realize that the gospel has afforded us hidden nuggets in these texts. Even though the scriptures have been dug through for countless centuries there is a healthy amount of gold left to be discovered. In the United States and abroad it is projected that 90% of the gold has been mined. I believe that we have only scratched the surface of the mining beds of the biblical text.

Lastly, I crave for every clergy to have a fighting chance, which would include all of those within the diversification of race to the indigenous cultural view of Christ within every nation. I would love to witness the reality of solidarity in pulpits across America. It is my belief that together we can all strike it rich within the Savior, Jesus Christ by offering enriching sermons. I only hope you've brought your empty sacks because there's a ton of gold hidden there in the text and it is yours for the taking.

Dr. Aaron L. Chapman

In Loving Memory of

Auntie Charlotte (Charlotte Thomas)

Momma Jackie (Jacquelyn Harper)

Dr. J H Ellens

Notable Mention

Faye Chapman (Mom)

Christopher Whitsett

Dennis Thorton

To My Family

Valarie Love you Honey Always

Aaron Shoot for your dreams

Destiny Keep Singing for the Lord

Introduction

Mining for Masterpieces

"Digging for another Dimension"

There is gold in them there homiletic hills . . .

It was with regularity in my embryonic years of preaching ministry that my Pastor, Tellis Chapman would always remind me to keep reaching and keep digging for more. This was his keen advice for a young aspiring preacher to "REMAIN HUNGRY"!

Since those fleeting moments there has been a stirring inside of me especially concerning the latter part of his advice, which was to "keep digging". I have laid with that thought, I have physiologically run countless miles with that looming language in my mind, I have allowed for it to brew and even boil over within me. There has been a noble nudging homiletically for me to unearth a system to express the audacity of clergy who seek precision and godly power while daring to craft a masterful sermonic portrait from an existing passage of scripture.

The internal inquiry or question that rises instantly from those intrigued by homiletic proficiency is; what is considered a masterful sermonic portrait from scripture? A sermonic portrait is crafted with spellbinding spirit; scholastic integrity and skillful art. Those aforementioned terms will be articulated as a masterpiece for our purposes in this text.

While pondering over the best course of action to arrange this text, I was privileged to visit Nashville Tennessee for a Preaching Conference. I was further honored to be the homiletics instructor for the conference and keynote preacher. One afternoon while seeking to pick up a nourishing meal from a local pub that was in close proximity of the hotel, I noticed an Art Gallery in the mini mall complex. I decided to stop in to take a glace at the artistic displays that I'd seen in my peripheral view during my morning jog earlier that day. I find it intriguing to experience and/or observe others who are masterful and exhibit greatness in their craft. While I was there I was exposed to paintings that were canvassed by Thomas Kinkade who is affectionately known as the "Artist of Light".

According to the distributor, Kinkade was known to use a plethora of paint tallying over a thousand brush strokes per portrait. These strokes created a different lighting affect when a person would view the painting at different angles and shades of lighting. I stood awe struck by the artistic dominance of Kinkade.

Those gleaming lights highlighted the gravity of his genius, which yielded the results of a masterpiece. I left there inspired and informed. These Emotions that surfaced in a novice observer of these paintings should not only surface when viewing extraordinary artistry such as those portraits, but even more so these powerful and overwhelming emotions should take place while congregants and skeptics experience the authentic art of preaching. Eugene Lowry affirms this thought process in his book entitled "Doing Time in the Pulpit" Lowry explains that Whether the artist has chosen the words or colors on purpose, or whether the words or colors seem to have chosen the artist, the result is that powerful experience that sometimes surprises not only the beholder but even the artist. Lowry further explained as Grady Davis exclaimed a sermon has a life of its own. (Lowry 1985, 90)

Shortly after having this tremendous experience in this art Gallery there was yet this ideational nudging about crafting a masterpiece in the pulpit work. Reflectively, I began reiterating to myself keep digging, keep digging. What was suddenly so urgent about this utterance? Why had this concept captured my cognitive energy and cease to let me go? I continued with what I deem as the norms of life; preaching, teaching and exercising etc . . . During a moment of homiletical training of a group of clergy I began to emphasize the importance of becoming familiar with the different layers of a text through casual observation; defining insight and exposure of the undergirding themes of the text; I further explained that the Bible can be likened unto mining and we are looking for nuggets, which can help craft, a masterpiece.

This inspirational moment lead me to the researching of the process of mining and I discovered that there were striking similarities to what is done in the pulpit compared to those whose profession is to excavate gold and diamonds from the clay coffers of the earth. This is the coordinate from which this concept mining for masterpieces was derived. There are so many clergy in the world who have mined for these masterpieces. As Thomas Long remarked that we are privileged to go into the caves of the text and explore all of the markings from homileticians of the past such as Irenaeus, Augustine and Dr. Martyn Lloyd Jones but the fascinating thing is that you have the opportunity to leave your ministering mark and probing gospel personality. The question remains will you leave something worthwhile to build on. I believe that as a chosen clergy you have something to offer the homiletic cave, so let's keep digging! Turn the page as we turn over the divine dirt of God's word to discover the masterpieces . . . I believe there is gold in those Homiletic Hills!

Chapter 1

Miners Perspective

A story was once told of an eager mining crew that ventured to a mountain to extract gold. To the delight of these determined diggers they quickly found a remnant of gold. Even though the source of gold was scanty they knew it would lead to a significant amount of gold. They continued digging attempting to mine larger quantities of gold but failed to excavate anything for weeks. The crew became discouraged and decided that there was no reason to continue because there were obviously no more resources in those mountains. The gold fever so to speak, was gone! Amazingly they left their tools and departed from the mountain with a sense of despondency.

A short time after, another energetic crew arrived at the same mountain as the former crew who were filled with despondency. They discovered a pick left in the ground where the former crew ceased from their digging and with just one striking blow, they hit the mother load of gold and they became millionaires! (I am not sure if there is much truth to the story but it has a moral lesson worth mentioning). The moral of this story is that when the first crew came to their wits end unbeknown to them they were just one more action away from an abundance of gold.

This story is very entertaining but we can also make a parallel to the homiletic homicide recapitulated by the heralds who won't hang in there when the text isn't immediately forth coming with revelatory information in the initial seating. Let me ask you, what text have you given up on? What text have you completely walked away from because it didn't appear to have any substance? What text have you tabled that was one turn of the page from yielding its life changing truths? Those sermons that you hear that are saturated with supernatural syllogisms are birthed from sweat equity within the corridors of a solemn study or tenacity exhibited while tarrying at a table. Preaching is Hard Work Period! Let me Exclaim that again! Preaching is Hard Work! Those who don't believe this might not be doing it correctly. The truism of this previous observation is exposed in the following statement of Elizabeth Achtemeier: "It takes work to know God through the bible that way—hard concentrated, sustained study and learning – care with the text and scholarly probing of its layers." (Achtemeier 1980, 38)

For you to endure the irritant of exegetically coming up empty, preaching must become who you are and not just what you do alone.

Donald Macleod reminds us in his book *The Problem of Preaching* that preaching is proclamation and it is witness. He further explains that Preaching is the art of making a preacher and delivering that (Macleod 1987, 35). Stephen Rummage who quotes Ramesh Richard says that 'Preaching should promote the integration of biblical truth with the living which becomes authentically Christian Preaching." (Rummage 2002, 41) T Harv Eker in his book *Secrets of a Millionaire Mind* asked the question, "What would it make of you to become a millionaire?" (Eker, 2005, 2). As you struggle and strain through scripture to give substantial life changing principles ask yourself the question; what would it make of you to become a great preacher? The answer . . . this type of dedication and digging is guaranteed to yield dazzling results.

Today in this evolving world of postmodernity, challenges are not well accepted, especially to gain access to the authenticity of biblical truth. The world has become enticed and encumbered with the ideology that everything must be saturated with simplicity to be deemed worthy of spending quality time. This consciousness has been birthed during the immense success of Macintosh's Apple Era. Apple has showcased their various products to simplify life and learning. This former critique does not insinuate that everything should be intrinsically complex to be deemed as valuable. Although I find this interesting, I encourage you to take note of how this concept has also shifted our religious cultural context because of these secular implications.

There are staunch defenders of postmodernity who consider those who reason and wrestle with theological issues in sermons to be causing unnecessary strain on them. They further concur that these interpretations should come naturally and lean toward a more experiential methodology of interpretation for each individual. In Martin Luther King Jr.'s text *"Strength to Love"* King appears to be oscillating between the concept of the soft mind versus the tough mind, he suggested the following about these endorsements of ease: "Rarely do we find men who willingly engage in hard, solid thinking. There is an almost universal quest for easy answers and half-baked solutions. Nothing pains some people more than to think." (King 1963, 14) Thomas Liske who cited Bishop Sheen concurred with the thoughts of Martin King by stating "These are days when ignorance is bliss and when tis folly to be wise." (Liske 1951, 222) He further states "The only people who can sleep these days are the ignorant who know not what goes on in the world."

Marvin Gaye, a Motown legend during the times of the thick tension and glaring riots in America used lyrical expression through song to express his feelings and the feelings of several others as he asked the question "What's Going On?" This is the earnest question that screeches from the streets contemporarily for every sermon to address. Unfortunately for some, it becomes a stalemate in the study of the clergy if they fail to sink their theological picks deep into the scriptures to retrieve the nuggets that put them on notice of the removal of a nebulous theological cloud thereby keeping them informed of what's going on. Be advised to achieve this end it takes much work! In a sermonic sense and through thoughtful reflection O C Edwards Jr. suggested there are two things that take time, the first is . . . studying the exegesis of the gospel and boning up. The second . . . There must be a lot of mulling over the fruits of your exegesis. (Edwards 1983, 21)

Unfortunately, there is no appreciation for an old fashion work ethic to dig for what is theologically, doctrinally and divinely desirable; most declaration has become fluff a type of cotton candy theology which goes in the spiritual mouth but dissolves quickly for the lack of solid substantive development. Presumably, there is no acknowledgement while going through the digging process that there is another preacher beginning to emerge within the preacher; this produces clergy who began to see that the method is just as important as the message. Technological advancement has been a blessing and a curse because through many of our software venues our creative thoughts in sermonic crafting have been kidnapped because they keep the cookies so low for everyone to create thoughtless trite cookie cutter sermons that suffice to the irritant ears (itching ears) and are devoid of a person's unique finger prints on a text.

Believe it or not, the preacher has to pay, but it beats compensating someone to craft sermons for keeping you in a corrupted, convicted, consciousness while injecting sermonic steroids to continue boosting ones stats and shouts on live streams; or surfing the web countless hours to find a sermon no one has possibly heard yet. The alternative is to do it the old fashion way and that is pray, or pick a passage of scripture and allow for providence to deposit the proclamation, or during persevering in study. Nevertheless, no matter how you do it, you will pay.

When a preacher prefers to dig for the meaning of eternal truths he denounces the careless observations that can be given to sacred text. The preacher further endorses that casual interpretive responses will not be sufficient and sustainable for the strong winds of newly ascribed theological trends.

Tools of the Trade

Preaching is Hard Work but it is even a tougher task when you don't have the proper tools in order to execute. An Early Church father of the Christian Faith St. John Chrysostom in Manchester England known as the "golden mouth" of preaching expressed these words concerning the burdensome task of preaching. "A minister of the word who writes about preaching writes as a learner to other learners and like them he is haunted by the sermon that no one is great enough to preach." (Fisher 1979, 73)

In the secular sense every profession or trade has its own tools. If you are seeking to have your car repaired it is a futile task if the mechanic or technician doesn't have at their disposal the right tools; A dentist that is going to do a routine procedure such as a root canal will not even start the finalization of the process if they don't have the cap; A roofer won't waste his/her time coming out to the job if there are no hammers nails, nail guns, and shingles to cover the roof because they need the correct tools to sustain their work so they can guarantee their work. Even technologically if you call into a corporation seeking information about an account or to make a payment and their computers are down they will request for you to call back! Why because they don't have the proper tools to assist you. Just as these other professions are in need of the proper tools, the preacher in the exegesis process needs worthy tools to capture a worthy word for awaiting listeners.

Elizabeth Achtemeier affirms this view in her text *Creative Preaching* when she wrote, "The committed preachers—the faithful servants of God – do not neglect their tools."(Achtemeier 1980, 22) Achtemeier further explains that "A preacher's tools are words, shaped into the rhythms and cadences the fortissimos and whispers, the conversation and confrontation of oral speech."(Achtemeier 1980, 22) To be effective in this herculean feat of heralding for heaven each week if done effectively clergy must have the correct tools. Just as the miner has set out in order to excavate gold the same type of planning must be implemented to procure the posits from the passage to craft a sermonic masterpiece. We have to be strategic in loading up the right tools prior to venturing to the sacred grounds. During the initial call of the preacher what a difference it would make to have a bucket list of the necessary tools required to load up for the ministerial journey. How many years could be saved detouring from wasted time for clergy if properly advised regarding their need for strong spiritual and academic tools?

To make the proper investment in resources there must be a concurrence in the conscious of the clergy that there is invaluable information that will be shared that will challenge, nurture, and expose the mind to information that will inspire well beyond the initial cost. The preachers deliberate and default text should always be the scriptures; while this should be emphatically expressed there are other books that should be considered. A preacher should consult classic novels, collegiate texts that deal with biology, American history, poetry, drama and sociology, these will also be extremely beneficial along with scholarly commentaries such as: Word Biblical Commentary; Interpreters Commentary; The Testament Library.

These are a few beaming benchmarks of where true expository biblical preaching should gain its focus and fuel. You must refuse to compromise when it comes to investing in spiritual tools.

A Note from Dad

My father Rev. Joseph Chapman always spoke of the innumerable ways that the right resource could impact my ministry. He called it your toolbox. He is a master builder and he would frequently take us to the tool outlet stores and we would have to sluggishly watch him look over tools and ponder over future projects. My father would literally select tools for a project he hasn't even started yet or may not start in the next five years! As I began to mature he explained to me that a multiplicity of tools were important because you never know when you'll need that tool for the tight spots. When I began preaching he explained in my embryonic years that tools are analogous to ministry equipment and that is you need to purchase books that you will not grow out of. What my father meant by this is don't get a book based on economic affordability. Preachers need to ask themselves for future projects will I need this. There are preachers that don't know the Greek or Hebrew language but the Novum Testamentum Graece is something that is invaluable for your library or the Biblia Hebraica you might not understand this now or you might have buried these books after seminary but when you need to see the original text you will have it at your finger tips which saves you time from traveling to the library for everything.

Experienced Miners Supply Warehouse

Most great preachers graciously lead new comers to the heralding spiritual process with bread crumbs liken unto the fictional characters Hansel and Gretel. They do this while they are teaching or preaching, but most estranged to the process don't ascertain what is transpiring because they are fans of preaching but not faithful followers of the homiletic craft.

One of the greatest investments a preacher can make is to be observant in the warehouse of the witness that has a wealth of knowledge and experience. Where is this warehouse you may ask? The answer, the preacher's or pastor's study.

Wallace Fisher exposes the relevance of this point when he stated "Too many preachers are lying down on the job . . . The time which they do spend among their books, or speak more accurately in the same room with their books—what do they do with it mostly they kill it. Few preachers kill time in their studies anymore. They do not have studies. They have well—appointed offices." (Fischer 1979, 95)

If a preacher has not arranged space in his office for serious scholarly study and spiritual reflection this is an indicator that they will have anemic observations to offer you concerning the accuracy of homiletics or hermeneutics. The serious student of the word surrounds themselves with treasured voices that render value.

One writer suggests the profundities of libraries are that they are literal living voices on the shelf that we can consult. What have become prevalent are miss opportunities in ecclesiastical gatherings. The greatest missed opportunity that a preacher has is when he/she speaks too much but does not scan the shelves enough in the experienced miners study. The preacher has left you clues of what picks and shovels have served him or her well through the years that will assist in advancing your ministry in the current day. There must be fingerprints from the past so that you can prophetically gaze forward with homiletic integrity for the future. It is a good rule of thumb that if there is disparity on the shelves it is an indicator there is disparity in the declaration.

One of the greatest pieces of advice that I received from Pastor Tellis Chapman was to seek out an older preacher, grab on to his suit jacket and put a wrinkle in it. This advice meant to hold conversations; have preplanned questions; pass to them well thought out sketches and outlines and be open to the scrutiny of the seasoned eye, and the golden years of wisdom. You need to hold on to the experience miner and with the intensity of Jacob wrestling the spiritual benevolent being and hoarsely repeating "I won't let you go until you bless me". There are too many postmodern preachers that are disrespectfully dormant they have no drive in their servitude or devotion in their care for the pioneers and pavers of preaching ministry. They fail to realize as Isaac Newton stated that "we are dwarfs standing on the shoulders of giants".

The last feeble portion of advice concerning the experienced miners is found in classic homiletic text. Seek out the fraternity and or sorority of preachers in print they will give you strong doctrinal material and theological insight that will enrich the landscape of your lens for perceiving pertinent hidden gems in the passage. These individuals can be academic or could have arisen from informal training both have invaluable information. These books could be pamphlets of sermon manuscripts that you scan for substance and structure, not to steal for sanctuary use on the next speaking engagement; or for those in academia to utilize in researching what was their theory toward preaching and how it has served them in the classroom and preaching in the midst of congregants.

There are several occasions where we can find mentors in books that can help us immensely on our ministerial journey. Every experience miner needs to have the respect and the reverence given by up and coming miners, which grants maintenance to experience miners in their latter years to preserve the dialogue. It breaks my heart to remember a time when Pastor Caesar Clark was in the middle of the National Baptist Convention halls in a wheel chair and I saw several young preachers walk by him intentionally. The weight of the years had wrinkled his countenance and weakened his frame therefore he had to seek stability in a wheelchair. I felt privileged that day for first being aware who he was but secondly to have the privilege to push the wheelchair of a preaching living legend. You cannot advance a wheel chair but one way and that is you must position yourself in the back. This must be the hearts desire of the mentee or understudy and that is to have their leaders back. There must be a collaboration for the experienced miners to know in the spring of the life of the inquisitive sermonizers there is a solid respect and reserved place in their heart to give and glean from their work.

Mapping out the Journey

Prior to engaging the sermonic process there must be a sense of location. For the miners in yester year to discover precisely where the trails and mountains for mining were they had to have a map. These sketches gave them a familiarity of the grounds prior to their arrival it also assisted them with insightful direction. In preaching the map would be the biblical text that you desire to use to get to the grounds of scripture. Ronald Allen affirms "A good map is invaluable when planning a long trip. In much the same ways a map of the homiletical terrain can help us preachers know where we want to go in a given sermon."(Allen 1992, 1) On one occasion while visiting a Bible bookstore I ease dropped on a dialogue between two inquisitive women concerning the choice of a Bible for their Sabbath day totting; this conversation emphasis was bathed in the preference of style and portable size rather than the substance between the golden or silver seals of the Bible.

Each preacher should know why they have selected a particular Bible and what purpose it will serve. Your initial thought should focus on what version of the Bible you're selecting. The selection of the translation of the Bible is significant to the accuracy of one's biblical exegesis. The space and time within this writing fails to allow me the time needed to appropriately and extensively layout the entire process of translation variations, therefore I will concisely highlight concepts necessary for selecting a Bible that will serve you well. There are different categories according to the method implemented to transfer the ancient wording in the manuscripts to the present reader. There is a word for word translation, which is within the NASB and NRSV. The next category is a paraphrase such as the Message Translation or the Living Translation. The word for word translation transacts the original language translated into its present form. These paraphrases are translations that are placed in the translators own wording. This is not an extensive explanation but a concise one concerning the move from transmission to translation which is spoken about extensively within the text *Grasping God's Word,* in order that the translators can cross the principled bridge from the ancient world to today's contemporary audience.

There needs to be a translation that you read with regularity so that you can employ an effective memorization and familiarity with the translation. It is preferable that the preacher selects a study Bible that gets as close to Jesus time as possible in the manuscript that is explored. In the seminary, I advise my students to purchase the NRSV Harper Collins Society of Biblical Literature Translation. This particular Bible is used by the scholars while engaging in biblical criticism (comparing and contrasting manuscripts)which helps with the accuracy of an exegete's interpretation. Another bonus of this text is the extensive introductory information and its commentary. Any serious clergy would find this to be an outstanding asset for hermeneutical precision. The importance of this is keeping the academic perspective before the student while they are engaged in a transforming spiritual exercise.

The vast importance of the biblical text should never be neglected and nullified for the embracing of niches rather than biblical truth. This can unfortunately lead to the critique of Fred Craddock in the cognitive scriptural understanding creating "The Dead Air of Familiarity" for whom attendance at worship is habitual. (Achtmeier

1980, 13) There must be an interpretive integrity that becomes the bread tie that consistently preserve the freshness of the scriptural text so that it does not become stale bread to veteran attenders but yet remain sterile in its aim for the newbies in the faith.

The Bible is one of the most important texts in the preachers' work. The Biblos or the spiritual library has bottomless depth of wisdom, which has served and will serve countless ages. Several homiletic minds have articulated the intrinsic value of the Bible. This biblical text Rhodes suggested of John Wesley after hearing the book of Romans quoted from Martin Luther stated, "His heart was strangely warmed and he was at peace with God." (Rhodes 2005, 263-264) Thomas Liske's, observation was that "The Bible is like a fair and spacious orchard in which all kinds of trees grow." In the text *Sermon without End*, it is articulated by the Allen's that "The Bible, it has been correctly said is the word of God given in human words in history. It is this dual nature of the Bible that demands of us the task of interpretation." (Wesley and Ronald Allen 2015, 21) In the Text *Creative Preaching* It is stated of Charles Spurgeon "Being converted by a preacher who lacking anything else to say constantly repeated his text. The smoldering word of God burned deeply into Spurgeon's heart and burst into unquenchable evangelical flame." (Achtemeier 1980, 12) It is through these sacred texts that we help congregants abandon the slippery slope of satanic heresy and accept the sustaining truths of God.

As we enter into ministry, none of us are privy to know how far and how fast God will accelerate our ministry. With that stated we have to make sure that we have two areas covered and that is the exegetical ammunition for home and our exegetical artillery for the road. There needs to be a priority given to a library that you are constructing at home. This is necessary because everyday there should be a desire and attempt to stretch beyond where you were the previous day. One obvious advantage that you have with having a library at home is the time in travel, which is traded off for the time that you could be exegetically executing turning your spare time into skill enhancing time. This library can be digital or it can be a hard copy but I believe that it speaks to the commitment of the preacher whose home life reflects his/her calling, passion, and pride in the lot that the Lord has casted over their life and the opportunity to build a legacy for the centuries to come.

Let me ask you a question if I did a site visit to your home could I tell what you do and what you live for? For those of you who protest this by saying leave the church at the church and home at home, let me raise this question: Why do NBA stars have basketball courts inside or outside of their homes? Why do Boxers have exercise rooms and quarters to store their belts on display? It is because they have discovered what they were born to do and it naturally is displayed in their environment. I must advise you that whatever is naturally displayed before you as a preacher is what and where you will devote the most time. The late Jim Rohn stated that "The issue is when we ought to play we are working and when we are working we should be playing." We should never mix the two because it could be to our detriment for others to assume that someone who is working cannot be taken serious because they play most of the time or when you take a vacation you're working when you need to play to avoid burnout." For any immature clergy that makes caricature of the faith, you must not know the pain permeating in the gospel if you are playing in the pulpit. Serious preachers take sacred things serious. When clergy have a designated environment/room/study it is time to go to work! Sense you are prepared to work, Let's turn the page and keep digging for more.

Chapter 2

Miners Pilgrimage

There is a detrimental hardship that happens to miners that are headed in the wrong direction to mine valued assets. Likewise for clergy who are not clear of what course of action they desire to take, they must dig to capture celestial clippings God has implanted in the text (they need not make up their own meanings) for congregants to move seamlessly from biblical clarification to impactful application through intentional excavation. To fulfill such a task, I believe that there must be a mindset of digging through the layers of the text as miners to strike the place where textual understandings yield a gold standard. Frequently when a preacher studies a text briskly there is yielded to him or her surface meanings and cloudy thought-out materials that may suffice for a shabby amen just to abruptly quicken the preacher's sermonic emergency landing. The process of discovering the core meaning of the text enamors studious preachers. The intriguing query that should be considered is; what principles are there that lies behind the casual observation that demands an investigative process to cut through the layers of biblical understanding?

These layers are not a search for esoteric encounters or outer space utterances. Gordon Fee warns against a false understanding of spirituality where the Bible is full of deeply buried truths waiting to be mined by the spiritually sensitive person with special insight. (Fee and Stuart 2003, 18) Rather there should be a pursuit for the central truths that ring with synchronicity with the cross embracing gospel of Christ. These are not just ideologies, these are not just endorsed methodologies; these are not some excrement expositions that profit us nothing cited by Paul in his letter to the church at Philippi in Phil 3:8 NASB, but a pilgrimage that is saturated with passion to unpack the principle that yield life altering truths. Gordon Fee and Stuart further suggest the aim of good interpretation is simple: to get at the plain meaning of the text. Even though there is solidarity in the motives of interpretation between my theological views and Fees, there is a separation concerning the layered meanings that are found below the surface. For some text there are too many unknown variables that surface reading will not yield its treasure, there has to be a skill, an art and science to seek reliable sources to render accurate norms of antiquity so they can be interpreted in the nagging domestic context.

Foreign Soil

As citizens of the United States whenever we venture out of the States they articulate other atmospheres as foreign soil. This phraseology refers to conditions, culture and climate that can be far different from what one experiences at home. No matter how often the scriptures have become visually apparent in our everyday world be it in hotels, courtrooms, and liturgies, the looming reality is when we crack the seal of the scriptures we are transported onto foreign soil. If we will fair well, we need to become acquainted with the soil. There are far too many ministers that are mining for masterpieces that have not taken the necessary time to grasp the importance of knowing the soil. Duvall and Hays speak to this in the text *Grasping God's Word*. In their text this gives the example of a traveler that is parachuted into a foreign country. This is their first time and they are at a lost because they are not familiar with the language, the geography, the customs and especially the cultural idiosyncrasies. This is analogous to our experience every time we open the Bible we have made the leap into another context and we remain sharp in our handling well the scriptures if we approach it as coming to the text for the first time. Familiarity sometimes breeds disrespect and whenever you are approaching a text if you take it for granted you can violate the text.

In the process of mining there is a harsh procedure called stripping the ground. This is when you mined a piece of earth with machinery and the digging is not to replenish or turn over the soil for more fertilization. This stripping is to retrieve from the soil what is there at any cost so that you can gain the treasure but leave a traumatic affect on the ground. When a minister that is mining a text is motivated by only what he can get out of it instead of the principles of God that is purposed to precede others on a spiritual journey they will engage in stripping. This stripping in Homiletics would be referred to as the process of eisegesis. When a person engages in eisegesis they look into the text or put preconceived ideas into the text. This is when the exegete has endorsed their first theology of their preconceived notions and assumptions without testing them. These exegetes strip the scripture of its meaning in order to satisfy their own separatist agenda.

The way that you can avoid stripping the grounds of scripture and closing the gap of being estranged from the original context is Exegetical Discovery (ED). Exegesis is the process of drawing out of the text what is there through using hermeneutical technique and other necessary study methodologies. Discovery is articulated as follows: The real voyage of discovery consists not in seeking new landscape, but in having new eyes. Discovery in the scriptures is not to acquiesce to ulterior truths of scripture that would be heretically using scripture as a hypothesis that leads you to your own higher thinking but the miner should approach the scriptures with a different or new set of eyes. I'm reminded that on one occasion as a child I decided to borrow my friend's prescription eyeglasses and wear them for the day. On the Playground things were very large and for a time it was fun until I begin to develop a migraine headache. I discovered that when I tried to look through someone else's prescription lenses it hurt me. An Optometrist that diagnoses a patient's diminishing sight in any way must prescribe new eyeglasses to allow them to see with clarity. I believe that the Holy Spirit is our Optometrist and he uses the tools or resources to bless us with new eyes to interpret the landscape of the text. The way that we get this done is through ED, Exegetical Discovery.

The Exegetical Discovery is initialized engaging. In the context here we will delineate it as testing the soil. The soil that I am referring to is the books of the Bible as a whole where you have discovered there are nuggets. As I view the scriptures from the miner's prospective, I compare the soil or bed to the entire book but each chapter is considered deposits or nuggets that are spread throughout the soil or book. If we are to have an effective pilgrimage as we make these exegetical discoveries we'll need more familiarization with the soil. The miner needs a couple of tools here: Introduction to the New Testament and or Old Testament; The survey of the Old and New Testament; etc . . . One of my favorites, Introduction to the New

Testament by Raymond E. Brown. The reason I ascribed to this particular introduction is because he wrote it for the access of laity and the scholar. This book will help to give a strong and detailed overview of the book as a whole oppose to commentaries that focus most of their energy and space to word studies, connecting homilies, manners and customs and syntactical repetition and structure. Brown explains his purpose below:

> First the readership that is envisioned has implications. This book is introductory, and therefore not written for fellow scholars. I envision both readers who have become interested in the NT on their own and readers who take NT beginning courses on different levels (e.g., Bible study groups religious education, college surveys and initial seminary classes). (Brown 2010, vii)

The use of this tool will have you to focus on the manuscripts of the scriptures. The manuscript are the writings of the original audience so that you don't strip the ground trying to force the scriptures into a contemporary context. The reason why this is important and I disagree with Fees argument for plain surface meaning is because as Brown suggested moreover some basic concepts of NT Theology (e.g., koinonia) defy adequate translation. This confirms that if we desire to hold to accuracy we must plan to dig and make our exegetical discovery.

Another source that is worth its weight in gold is the Survey of the Bible I have enjoyed the indelible impact the New Interpreters Bible Survey has had on my Theological perspective. The survey assisted in exposing the preacher to various in-depth content such as, literary context and the historical context through scholarly essays and or journals. Leander E. Keck explains:

> While it is appropriate to distinguish historical and literary explanation of the text as a work of the past from reflection on its import in various situations today, it is also necessary to ground the later in the former . . . . what effective and imaginative interpretation needs most is solid grounding in an explanation of the text that engages the religious and moral content of scripture. (Keck 2005, v)

The obvious question for those who have not been initiated to these terms or a refresher to those who need to remove the dust from proper recall is what is the historical and literary context? The historical context is very elusive for the scholar and non scholar Michael Gorman suggest that the historical context is Reconstructing the historical contexts of the biblical writings "Occasion" (Gorman 2009, 71). The literary context is comparable to the reconstruction of a crime scene. Prior to the arrival of the detective the crime scene is closed off with caution tape. The reason why the area is secluded is because the detective doesn't desire anything to be tampered with. The detective is adamant about this because time has elapsed between the occasion and or event. The detective's objective is to reconstruct the event focusing on the accuracy of how it transpired. The preacher's weekly assignment is to be a homiletic detective. When the ministry miner investigates these texts they are trying to reconstruct the events so that they can reach the original meaning. This process makes it achievable to transfer the meaning from the ancient time to the contemporary context.

The literary context is also expressed as a context plural. The image of the literary context would be three intersecting circles, which have the larger context as one and the immediate verses before and after as the other two. Gorman refers to these as, concentric circles of the literary context. (Gorman 2009, 71)

When the miner is digging for this information, there is a recreating of the scriptural scene and setting. Historically there is a reconstructing of the location and those in power politically (government) and ecclesiastically (church). Then the literary context is what were the conversations and or events that took place as the details between the larger narratives. As you are mining you must search for the principles that are most pertinent to the meaning that God has to direct and guide a congregant's daily activity and decision making. If we don't dig for this information it will result in uninformed enthusiasm and our job is not to motivate here but to uncover the meaning. Just motivating is dangerous business. Jim Rohn stated on one occasion that "if you want to get a guy going just motivate him". Then Jim Rohn asked what if he is an idiot then you have a motivated idiot and you don't want that.

The purpose of familiarizing yourself with the soil or bed is so that you can be sure that you've arrived at a specific ground and not the grounds of generality. The Bible has a makeup of specific genres. They have been categorized in several ways but here's a basic list: Narrative, Psalms, Proverbs, Apocalyptic Gospels, Epistles etc . . . There is a reason for this because it assists the miner in knowing where to dig in order to get to the assets that they are after. The worst thing that could happen is for you to dig expecting to find gold but you then discover that instead of finding gold you've been digging in a place where there are diamonds. They are both valuable and profitable but are they beneficial for your original cause. According to 2 Timothy 3:16 KJV, all scripture is given by inspiration of God and profitable for doctrine, for reproof, for correction, for instruction in righteousness. When the Spirit of God leads you in a certain direction it would be wise to remain in the vein in which God has inspired you. The question is, what burning concept has been churning? There is such a thing as something being profitable but not being proper for your present purpose to remain pure to the passage.

All scripture is proper but when being placed in an ill-advised vein violates its profitability it is not proper. Now some may be thinking "but it is the scriptures, the authority of the scriptures". William Shakespeare reminds us that the devil can cite Scripture for his purpose. (Gorman 2009, 69)

Something Foreign in the Soil

During a Christian Education seminar on relationships given by my beloved mother Faye Chapman, she informed us to beware of the critters! The real life illustration that she gave was brilliant she explained how she was an avid collector of plants and this began after she had been given several plants, one of which was given to her when my grandfather Willie Jim Thomas passed away (he died on my birthday). Mom further explained that she saw her plants dying and was wondering what was causing it? She watered them as needed and made sure they were placed in direct sunlight throughout the house to tickle the leaves with solar warmth but they continued dying. As this was transpiring she began noticing there were a lot of little bugs flying around the house, they seemed to appear suddenly and out of no where. She'd killed one and took it to the botanist to examine. They explained to her that those gnats were infesting and multiplying within all of the plants and when she examined the soil she discovered that they were right! The only way to keep the plants alive was to take each plant outside shake off all of the dirt surrounding the roots, wash the roots off thoroughly and then transplant them into new soil.

In our pursuit of reaching the different layers of the meaning, you may find that there are unscholarly sources, gnats or critters (intentionally or unintentionally) that can contaminate a preachers' theology. All in the name of being better than another preacher or in an effort to act as though they have something the others don't. They retreat to erroneous, heretical, false doctrines that is killing their ministry and moreover, it also causes a withering away of the faith of those who have to deal with the lack of Christ Centered and Christ Exalting Preaching.

There are ways to avoid this practice by seeking out the publishers that have a mission to express the importance of the inerrancy, infallible nature of scripture. Publishers such as: Zondervan, Eerdmans, Bakers, Varsity, Moody, and B&H are just to name a few. These publishing companies have stood for biblical integrity throughout the years. Avoid bargain bins unless it is for a reference book. Avoid anemic looking commentaries with no references and lastly look at the bio of the author. Where did they attend school? These are some helpful hints but still do not purchase it until you have looked at the parenthetical references or bibliography.

Motivation for Mining

Recently while on Facebook, a social media outlet I submitted my daily post on homiletics which stated: Sermons are developed when the preacher is developed. Preachers who are anti-education formally or informally are dangerous. When preachers who are entrusted with biblical truth, correct doctrine and solid theology are becoming endangered spiritual species these urgent times are damningly dangerous. These manipulative miners fail to realize it is very dangerous to discount homiletically the distance between the digging and the development of the sermon.

The term digging in this section will refer to research, which gives you resources that you can use to compliment an existing homiletic idea. The emphasis initially should not be on peripheral sources it should be on the self. James Finely affirms this in his book *Wake up and Preach*. He states "But—we are discussing the First Thing you the preacher should do approaching any occasion of preaching. You should go inside yourself not outside".

There are so many preachers trying to become somebody and there is a lack of trying to save someone (somebody) from their rascality. This is the symptom of destination disease. John Maxwell once wrote that what is most important is not the destination it is the journey. Miners of biblical truth I believe ascend from the ashes of their situation to grasp the hand of greatness. This is confirmed through a lecture given concerning Dietrich Bonhoeffer at the AOH (Academy of Homiletics): Preaching against the Idolatry of Nazi's. It is said of Bonhoeffer's climate. They provided rich soil for Nazism to take place. Bonhoeffer was not prominent he was a voice crying in the wilderness concerning Nazi power. There is an underestimation of how far clergy miners have to travel on their pilgrimage prior to them being endorsed by destiny to walk into the maximization of where your hour (passion) will take you in ministry. The sole motivation of taking shovel and pick to the grounds of scripture is to crave clarion understanding of the text to become an ecclesiastical informant of our inclusion in this incredible love story of the Gospel.

Chapter 3

Miners Process

Recently I have discovered that the same question is being raised cross—denominationally within the ranks of the clergy: Is there really an importance to considering the preaching style or form that I implement? This question has been offered in classrooms; preaching conferences; preaching roundtables; even in informal conversations while clergy chat about the previous days preaching efforts. There are particular homiletic professors that ascribed to the ideology that there is only one sermon style while others refute this view and affirm there are various styles.

To engage a clarion understanding of this books perspective; it would be advantageous for us to examine momentarily the word sermon. This word sermon comes from the Latin word sermo, which means speech. I would objectively cater to this personal addendum and delineate it as the spiritual speech since there are different types of speeches whether as a form of entertainment, to educate or persuade.

With the inescapable understanding that the Bible is its own sacred literature with various intrinsic genres, which are presented to various listening bodies, therefore there is practically a need for different sermon types or forms.

As anointed announcers assess the homiletic climate, I believe there is rarely a consideration that different forms used on a pericope could be more user friendly than attempting to force a form used regularly. Some of the reasons that some preachers may use one style is because 1). They have never been officially introduced to others 2). They have the mindset that if its not broke don't fix it or 3). Their fear of re-educating themselves in new ways of preaching and they find ways to justify it, all the while saving face and covering up their fear of becoming a student again. No matter what the phobias or the conscious claims that are made to commit to that one style; the question that must be ask is, is there potential and or preaching possibility that'll never see the light of day because their decision to change won't be deterred? During this Isolated, instance I want to impress upon you that there are other usable sermon forms.

Unfortunately, time will not allow me to articulate in-depth the different sermon forms but they are useful. Here is a quick running list of those you'll find: Textual, Topical, Narrative, Exposition, and Expository. For our time in this Chapter it is my desire to attempt to install a handle to the form of expository preaching so that it is useful to pour meaningful and potent principles into those listening which will help the preacher and pew both obtain progress.

There are those that have abdicated even the attempt of defining expository preaching. While others have endorsed and engaged in a sincere effort to take hold to a homiletic hypothesis and embrace what they're able to hash out as their classification of expository preaching. I'll say with some caution that I believe there should be a courageous effort to communicate and or define what is Expository preaching. Even though I agree with the late Haddon Robinson who suggested attempting a definition becomes sticky business because what we define we sometimes destroy. (Robinson 2001, 21) When this is done it allows for us to quickly identify what expository preaching is not. When we leave open the shed of subjectivity to an expository sermon any neophyte can claim that he or she has conquered the Mount Sinai of Expository preaching and there can be no decent objection because there was no dedicated time invested in defining it. The late Zig Ziglar stated that "you can never hit a target that you don't see" and I believe when we take the time to define expository preaching we will have some sense of if we've hit the target.

The depth and density of the substantive characteristics of Expository preaching has the connectors liken unto a loose-leaf notebook. There are several sheets of paper that make up the whole of the sermon but there are pieces that can stand on their own.

There are perforations installed which indicates that some parts of the documents are portable and can be connected in other places. This is what transpires when other text are supporting proofs to which provides further illumination and offer focus on a single text. There are those who give invaluable homiletic advice concerning expository preaching therefore, lets shift our attention to their excellent experiential findings

Here are some working definitions of Expository preaching:

Charles Koller "Expository Sermon consists of Exposition plus application and persuasion (argumentation and exhortation) . . . looking toward some form of response, in terms of belief or commitment." (Koller 1964, 21)

Haddon Robinson "Expository preaching is the communication of a biblical concept, derived from and transmitted through a historical, grammatical, and literary study of a passage in its context, which the Holy Spirit first applies to the personality and experience of the preacher, then through the preacher, applies to the hearers." (Robinson 2001, 21)

F.B. Meyers "Expository preaching is the consecutive treatment of some book or the extended portion of scripture on which the preacher has concentrated head and heart, brain and brawn over which he has thought and wept and prayed, until it has yielded up its inner secret, and spirit of it has passed into his spirit." (Rummage 2002, 78)

Harold Bryson "An Expository Sermon may be defined as a sermon in which the subject and the structure of the preacher's message reflect the subject and the structure of the passage of scripture." (Rummage 2002, 75)

William Taylor "By expository preaching I mean that method of pulpit discourse, which consists in the consecutive interpretation, and practical enforcement, of a book of the sacred canon. (Rummage 2002 78)

The Working Definition that I want to use for Expository Preaching is:

Dr. Aaron Chapman "Exposing Eternal meaning through exegetical contextual connection and interpretation."

The preacher must become a textual tell a tale for them to exhibit integrity and accuracy in the demanding field of expository preaching. We must give aligned axioms that expose eternal principles.

The structural bases for expository preaching perfectly supports the imagery of the miner that must remain discipline and exhibit patience to expose the treasure the text has to offer. What the text offers is not merely an infatuation with the inscriptions of dusty plagued dialogue of divine do's and don'ts but rather the authenticity of the imago Dei (image of God) that lies beyond our dust and is revealed by putting forth the effort to dig through the dust to affirm what has already been ordained. Dale Carnegie once stated that "We should treat people like we're mining for gold, you remove a lot of dirt to get an ounce of gold, but you don't go in looking for the dirt."

Dale Carnegie's observation is stirringly true. There are staunch defenders of that which is new and are vehemently demonizing the old religious order. Within this postmodern prospective they are adamant to discredit the mined dirt of scripture. They challenge the wiggling connectors of the narrative that are discourse that appears dislocated which then leads to a disinterest. The question of the authorship that looms over the ancient backdrop, verifies the challenge to its authoritative position and acceptance of these writings as truth. Those who stand in opposition to biblical inerrancy also question the similarities of the Christian story with other ancient writings that have arose among other religious types such as the Hebrew Israelites which challenge the mining fields of scripture. I still believe there is gold in those homiletical hills but it will require a godly faith and a thorough methodology to filter through the dirt to get to the noteworthy nutritious nuggets of the text in the words of Clifford Mayes.

Expository preaching offers us the possibility to involve ourselves in this inexhaustible effort of digging. The tools used in the process of mining gives us a methodology that will help us hit the mark of a meaningful sermon.

Pick the Scripture

The first item that is of importance in Expository preaching is the pick; there are four concepts that we should consider in order to obtain the best and most beneficial exegetical experience. The initial phase is *Picking the Scripture.* Selecting how much text your going to scoop out for a preaching presentation prior to crafting the message is essential. Jay Adams suggested through investigative inquiry "What, then is the determining factor? The purpose? You may preach on any purpose unit (text)—regardless of its length. Purpose is what defines a preaching unit" (Adams 1982, 26). As the preacher practices picking the scripture based on purpose, it forces the preacher to ask pertinent questions to arrive at such a spiritually conscious evaluation.

A couple of prospective questions may be: Does this sermon demand a singularity in its emphasis or a plurality? Does God want this theme repeated in successive sermons or in a single one? Are the versus capturing the contextual content necessary to give the congregants a solid base to sit with the text, struggle with the text and stride toward using the strategies implied by the text. Thirdly, we must have an introspective question; what is God doing in me and how much am I capable of collecting as a preacher before I become confused about the direction of the sermonic claim (sermon purpose)? Each sermon uses the purposeful limits in the text as a footing, this is the supportive element of the foundation that keeps the structure of the sermon solid and sturdy. In the Biblos of Matthew 7:24-27 Jesus Christ gives a parable of two men that built a house. One developer in futility built his house on a foundation of sand but the other built his structure or house on a rock, which is known as a footing, which is not easily shifted or moved.

When there is indeterminacy in the selection of the text limits the sermon can be easily shifted and the meaning ascribed becomes inconsistent and interpretation loses focus. The historical example of this is the Leaning Tower of Pisa in Italy. This monument is a unique tourist attraction based on its 10-degree leaning appearance, but it has not toppled over. The storyline behind the Leaning Tower of Pisa was that the foundation was not built to withstand the amount of weight placed upon it. When we are crafting from a pericope there is only so much that that sermon can hold before it has the possibility of falling apart. It is only by God's grace he has made some of our blunders into masterpieces and monuments in the faith even through our mistake of failing to secure the limits of its purpose.

Using the purpose to guide the selection will alleviate wasted energy on developing division of scripture that are interesting but not impactful for the particular purpose of the sermon. Which suggest that every scripture that is added doesn't mean that it advances the sermon toward its original intent that resides in the mind of the miner that is digging for the message. The preacher's role is analogous to Deutero Isaiah's goldsmith, there is a need to take the anvil and the hammer and smooth things out in our sermon and the first part is choosing with purpose. There are texts that are so vast. These text for the purpose of the sermon need to be limited in its usage based on the designated time for declaring the word of God. The technique to select the scripture is questioning the irrevocable call for action in the text. Preachers make a pick! Don't create spiritually inflated procrastination. Frequently there is a vagueness that plagues the preacher's observations in their expository pulpit work. Habitually vacating the decision to create limits for a text leaves discourse dangling out there opposed to demonstrating divine power through declaring his word.

Pick the Sacred Shifts

Every nugget of gold that you mine has peculiarity. One cannot maximize their time or mine gold efficaciously if they get obsessed with one piece of gold for an extended period of time. Let me express from the outset concerning eternal truths that these re-splendid revelations and providential principles of reason could last scriptural seekers a lifetime. As you are digging you must dig beyond the one nugget and with expectancy move on to the next one because there are sacred shifts that are happening within the soil through the grammatical function, the grouping of formulas and the gathering of frequent phrases.

After we have identified the sacred shifts these become our points that we are willing to take through the process of refining so that they may be revealed in the sermon. During a class on hermeneutics I was asked to expound on the scriptural information for their selected text. I offered an analogy of going to a clothing store and discovering there's a sale. There are not many people who will mindlessly put together a shirt and pants ensemble and then retreat toward the register for check out. No, there becomes a process of elimination based on the occasion for which you are going to wear this outfit. When we are selecting sacred shifts or points in the sermon we are engaged in dressing the sermon for a specific occasion. The last thing that you need is to overdress for the occasion, which attracts undesirable and or unnecessary attention. When we expose too much in the text for one sermon and not become selective we can overdress the sermon and instead of them focusing on God they are focusing on the dressing of the sermon.

There must be a theological wheel barrel that we bring to the text and load it with unnecessary utterance for a particular sermon. My mentor Dr. Abraham Smith offered me some impeccable advice and that was "Ask yourself, will it hurt them (The congregants) if you don't say it or will it help them (The congregants) if you do?" These priceless points focusing on unloading unnecessary utterances has served me well for almost 2 decades of homiletic crafting and meaningful mining to make sure I clearly think through the goal of the sermon.

The biblical accounts that illumines the text and extinguishes our disintegrating spiritual illiteracy is the telos. The telos in scripture signifies the purpose; the objective; the overarching goal of the scripture. In the text *Preaching with Purpose*, Adams suggested "There are few deficiencies in preaching quite so disastrous in their effect as the all–too-frequently occurring failure to determine the telos (or purpose) of a preaching portion." (Adams 1982, 27) When there is an ignoring of the telos there is enigmatic assertions given as sacred shifts (or preaching points) that never take hold of what the authors telos prescribed. When this menacing homiletic activity happens you can miss God's messaging minerals that should be communicated to the hearts of men and women while mining for the sermonic possibilities. Preachers don't miss God on the porch of the text while your trying to make it to the lower level of the textual housing.

Fortunately there is an endorsement from other homiletic professors who agree that there are different levels of the telos or the tele that resides in a text. This yet again verifies that the meaning of the text is found in the different layers of a text. The understanding of this substructure is that telos has different ranges so there is an original telos or purpose then there is a sub telos, and a sub, sub telos then the preaching portion (Adams 1982, 24). This reveals the inexhaustible nature of our task because I believe in eternity, God has an intended meaning for the unborn who will come to know him through these levels of telos/purpose that will cause them to clarify their internal individualistic purpose which connects to God's collectivistic plan for society.

Pick the Surroundings

During my research of the miner's methodology of exposing those materials within the earth; I discovered that there are dimensional variances to mining. There is above ground mining and there is under ground mining. This is to suggest that there are two sides to the effort to excavate the sought after material. Just as there are two sides in mining there are also two sides in almost every text with the exception of Gen 1:1 and Rev 22:21 even though contextually there are two sides.

In the discourse that you are mining or engaging in exegesis there is a need for a critical examination of the textual sides, the verses that precede it and the verses prior to it. I spoke earlier about how this creates a context but I want to go a little further. These text have the possibility of becoming sermons that were not even considered when the first observance of the text transpired. Pastor A. Louis Patterson Jr. use to verbalize that there was verses shouting out to him preach me too. There are those who struggle in their weekly regiment to come up with what to preach and they aren't looking in the pockets. They fail to see the gold that's hidden there and is anxiously waiting for the miner to bring the meaning to the surface.

During the initial years of mining gold, gold could be found flowing down stream by utilizing a pan. Which suggest that there is some gold on the surface of the earth. There are passages of scripture that literally have the gold on the surface. The preacher need not reconstruct and dig up what is there to create a telos or purpose of the text when the outline has been clearly given on the surface. Particular passages of scriptures that tend to have the gold on the top are the Epistles of Paul. Paul who used his expertise of constructing rhetorical arguments structurally gives you the sacred shifts of the text. One just needs to echo the eminent explaining and add exclaiming proclamation through personality and making it applicable to the pew or audience.

Balance is pivotal to understanding how you should construct the sacred shifts in a sermon. The preacher must determine when the text calls for literal interpretation and then when the preacher has to dig beyond the surface to grasp a keen theological understanding that will only set him or her up to choreograph the kerygma contemporarily for acceptable consumption. For literalism of interpretation Gordon Fee was correct when he stated "The aim of good interpretation is simple: to get at the plain meaning of a text" (Fee 2003, 18). For other homiletic scenarios it takes more then casual racking the ground of the text it takes a colossal amount of prayer, reading and research. Duvall suggest for this approach to deeper meaning that "Before we are ready to apply that meaning of (ancient context) to our lives (our town), we'll need to measure the width of the river that separates us from the world of the text (ancient text)." (Duvall 2012, 21) He further suggested "Most Christians however, desire to understand all of God's Word, not just the easy portions. Many of us want to be able to dig deeper into that Word." (Duvall 2012, 39). These are two examples of how we need to mine the Gold of Scripture there is surface gold and there is gold that you have to dig up to grasp it.

The surrounding passages of scripture that make up the context most times become a banishing of the present passages blind spots.

Numerous times an interpreter can read a passage repetitively and they are convinced that there is something missing. The thematic purpose of the scripture is illumined when there is a proper feedback that is channeled through the supportive surrounding scriptures.

Another practice that the preacher can engage is observing how the author has created the stories that he's placed comparison and contrasting narratively or in the storylines. There are conclusive events to the narrative that transpire at the end of an episodic encounter. The reason that the outcome is delayed is because it crystalizes the climax from the initial story so that it gives a well-rounded understanding of the telos as to why this narrative was placed strategically in the biblical order. This aforementioned method is used by Mark 11:12 when hermeneutically dealing with the cursing of the fig tree; the temple visit is also mentioned but then at the end of the story the fig tree is found withered from the words of Jesus the prophet. Concerning this withering . . . some scholars suggest it also represents the destruction of the temple.

For the purpose of sermon crafting, we are digging so that we can create a masterful display to reflect the incredible wisdom and profound nature of the scripture in the manuscript with a masterpiece quality.

Kobe Bryant, former Los Angeles Laker when speaking of the craft of basketball stated "everyone has a canvas in this life and it is up to you how creative you are with that canvas." This is what God has allotted through the power of personality for each of us. We are to take our homiletic canvas and take the conceptual colors of theological understanding and proclaim it to congregants through pronouncing or printing.

There are other tools that we will explore later within the upcoming chapters that will yield to us a soothing of our yearning to operate efficiently in the craft of expository preaching.

We've dug tirelessly in this chapter. Can you feel the soreness in your homiletical shoulders and the foreign soil between your nails? Lets take a break and reflect on what we have learned from this chapter and prepare to get back at it. I believe God's favor is upon us.

Chapter 4

Miners Power

Prayer is a vital part of the preparatory process of preaching. Prayer has been described by William Carey as; "Prayer — secret, fervent, believing prayer—lies at the root of all personal godliness." (Foster 1998 33) Clergy must remain cognizant that preaching is a spiritual impartation. O. C. Edwards suggest, "there is no point in preaching if you do not believe in praying." (Edwards 1982, 22) Frequently some clergy believe that if they are not fellowshipping within the orbits of Pentecostal denominationalism while affirming the experience of the outbreak during the Azusa Street Revival, then preaching with the Spirit doesn't apply. The acknowledgement of the Spirit is pivotal to ministering with personality, persuasion and power. Greg Heisler explained our sermon preparation and sermon delivery must be intentionally and prayerfully carried out under the leadership and power of the Holy Spirit. (Heisler 2007, 4) The Epistle John speaks of the importance of the modus operandi of filtering faith through effective witness in 1 John 4:1 *"Dear friends, do not believe every spirit, but test the spirits to see whether they are from God, because many false prophets have gone out into the world." (NASB)*

The Preacher must be willing to lose control. Preaching and creativity belong together and preaching is only authentically creative when illumined by the Spirit. (Wilson 2004, 2). Heisler is in agreement with Wilson when he stated "The preacher is Spirit driven, Spirit led and Spirit dependent will also be Spirit empowered. (Heisler 2007, 4)

There are a lot of areas in which the preacher can express responsible behavior such as putting aside study time; caring for the body through exercise, learning words to implement for vocabulary enhancement; or even attending a seminar or theological school, but none of this should be a substitute for the Spirit. These purposeful practices mentioned prior are sources that assist in Spirit lead preaching but not the sine qua non of preaching. From my feeble observation, Spirit *lead* preaching has become a lost art because of the lack of prayer. As the minister ministers they should be first ministered to prior to ministering. In Eugene Lowry's text *Doing Time in the Pulpit,* Water K England explains: "When the work takes over then the artist is enabled to get out of the way so as not to interfere. When the work takes over, then the artist listens." (Lowry 1985, 16) Moreover, it was also expressed: A sermon is not a thing at all; it is an order form of moving time. The one who makes sure that the sermon is moving in the right direction is the one who is spiritually led by personal intercessory prayer.

How appropriate is the testimony of Terry Wardle in his text Draw close to the Fire? He passionately explained: "Paul told the Corinthians that the Lord is the Spirit and where the spirit of the Lord is there is freedom (2 Corinthians 3:17)." I have learned that every moment I surrender to His Lordship, I am free to embrace that indescribable gift of Spirit life." (Wardle 1998, 51)

Prayer enveloped in the sermon parallels with the functionality of the electrical breaker box installed in a residential home. Without it there is structure but there is simultaneously no source of sustaining power. This calls to mind a recent warm sunny day; while my wife was charging her phone in the electric outlet built into our island of our kitchen a serendipitous event occurred. The charger was slightly loose in the outlet and her phone's case chain got caught between the outlet and the chain and there was an electric spark and the outlet or plug was disabled. I did not know that the outlet was disabled until I attempted to initiate a charge with my phone and received no power. I asked my wife did she know the plug was not functioning she explained what transpired with the case and the charger. She told me I needed to contract an electrician to have the plug repaired. I explained to my wife that prior to making this repair call I would first analyze the settings in the electrical breaker box. After a careful observation I began clicking the breakers back and forward and the plug began operating normally and has worked fine ever since.

This story is more than about making sure you have a compatible phone case and tightly plug chargers but it is a meaningful metaphor of what prayer means to the structure of the sermon. The breaker box is prayer and if there is no prayer there is no power that can connect to the necessary places to allow people to plug into the power of God. The sermon should not be a serendipitous transaction soaked in the lack of spirituality. Absolutely not! The sermon should be habitually housed with Holy Spirited directed prayer and power. F. Laubach has said "it is the preachers business to look into the very face of God until he aches with bliss."*

Each sermon if preached with power should be marked fragile handle with care. The mining process of obtaining a masterpiece is a process that has to be handled with care. The word of God is a precious document that has withstood the battering questions of history but the believers while they are handling the text should be conscious that the contents are irreplaceable and we should consider handling it with care. The miners of Scripture can't treat this document as one that is deceased but we are resuscitating the scriptures for present day congregant's curiosity.

Throughout the historical practices of mining; an enormous

number of miners attempted to retrieve gold from the belly of the earth they begin executing innovative excavating explosions to create passage under ground. The issue was that they didn't take the necessary steps to reinforce essential areas that were now vulnerable. This lack of knowledge was the cause of several cave-ins. There were other environmental hazards such as rock explosions. In addition water that forced itself into that open space made mining dangerous because there wasn't proper channels developed to handle the power of the excavation process. Believe it or not there are those that dig into the text and they've not stopped to dialogue with God, to ask Him to spiritually guide them through the scriptures. This can transpire when the miner or clergy has never seen their paradigmatic preacher engage in prayer. It is heart breaking for me to admit that one of the last line items of the agenda of most preachers is prayer. Richard Foster suggested that Prayer catapults us onto the frontier of the spiritual life. "Of all the Spiritual Disciplines prayer is the most central because it ushers us into perpetual communion with the Father." (Foster 1998, 33)

Let me ask you bluntly, do you pray as a preacher? Prior to you using your methodologies and downloading your ideologies on the text do you even seek the Holy Spirit for what God wants you to speak in the sermon? If this is not personally enforced prior to digging we leave gaps that are not reinforced that only can be filled with the Spirit of God. The Holy Spirit's guidance is an intrinsic part to the homiletic process. This is the gold detector that we need to give us permission and authorization to dig in the area that we are considering for sermonic delivery.

A homiletic prof impressed upon his students that "the Holy Spirit is the true communication in preaching. Preachers might be tempted to conclude that preaching is a gift that one either has or does not have. (Wilson 2004, 114) Karl Barth emphasized "there was no room for art or method concerning form in preaching or anything that would stand between the word and the congregation." (Wilson 2004, 114) Paul Scott Wilson stated "Peter had the greatest sermon in history with the greatest results in history and had no credits on his transcript in the area of homiletics."

I can remember very vividly the conversations with my father following every one of my preaching assignments, he would always eloquently verbalize the Apostle Paul's lively linguistic found in 1 Thessalonians 1:5 NRSV which states *because our message of the gospel came to you not in word only, but also in power and in the Holy Spirit and with full conviction.* The reason my father constantly explained this to me was because he wanted to remind me as a young preacher that book sense needs to be married with a bold spirituality; this indicated that I had to definitively depend on what was divine to get me through the days, dialogical sermo (Spiritual Speech).

The Holy Spirit's influence on the homily is an exercise of active listening. This is why Fred Craddock emphasis in his P301 the introduction to preaching was the ear and the mouth: to learn to listen (Craddock 2011, 6). During the years in which I was enrolled at Eastern Michigan University I was registered in a communications class entitled "Listening". One of the many lessons that were covered on the syllabus was active listening. During this lesson the professor differentiated between hearing and active listening. When you are just hearing your senses are activated by external stimuli from sound or noise but there is no focus necessary on the substance of the conversation. You heard it but you are not listening to it. The professor further explained that you could detect that someone is engaged in active listening when they're able to repeat back to you what you have said in great detail. Another proof of active listening is when there are questions that are prompting one to expose further insights.

When the preacher is digging for nutritious nuggets that will be proclaimed when he or she is lead by the Spirit, there is an asterisk next to it that has subject to change. This asterisk when relying on the Spirit takes place in the digging stage and in the dialogue stage in the homiletic process. The digging stage is in private study but the dialogical stage is in public worship. Those who dare to preach a dangerous sermon, as Frank Thomas would articulate it can't do such a monumental task on mundane methodology. It must be through meditation to receive an impactful message that presents a relevant word that revolutionizes the persons thinking and their treading; their perspective and how they progress; also their mindset and their mobility. The Spirit of God, the Pneuma in the Greek or the Ruah as the Hebrew word possesses the wind needed to take the fragile sermonic skeletons and breath life into them. So that dead skeletal outlined bones can live while preparing for God to place flesh on them from insightful interjections and the collection of scholarly voices in expectation for the sermo to stand in the sanctuaries across America as a mighty army.

Exegetical Explosions

In the historical documentary *Modern Marvels Mining for Gold*, this documentary informed listeners that during the mid 1800's there was a discovery of gold that was on the surface of the land in the Carolinas. The miners made their way from far and wide to attempt to tap the veins of the mountains to retrieve gold. This venture transitioned their focus from surface mining to underground mining efforts. This strategy of mining would allow miners to gain more gold deposits but it also increased the danger of the voyage.

Just as these miners ventured to these various places beneath the earths surface for more healthy sums of gold; the same behavior traits plagues the preacher who desires to gain deposits that have been divinely established by God in the veins of the text. There are several individuals that can interpret from a literary perspective but there is another element that I believe that goes beyond the wording of the text and that is the revelation that you receive from the Spirit of God while you are engaged in exegesis. This revelation is very different from an uninformed guess or hypothetical heresy hued in the homily concerning the passage because clergy have not invested the quality time or materials necessary to draft exegetical thoughts that have precision, practicality, personality and power and that can only be found through the Spirit. In some religious prospective, particularly in the Black Church, the Holy Spirit's activity is mainly described through demonstrative shouting but many seldom speak about the Holy Spirit being a huge influence during their study time. This isn't to say that this is all Black Churches which unfortunately one might assume because of what is reflected in the injurious stereotypical perfunctory presentation rendered by what I call shameful sitcomacalism. But there are some who know the third authority in Tertullianism as the triune God the Holy Spirit. The Spirit is active in the assignment of anointed preaching.

Jesus informed his disciples in John 14:26 *"But the Comforter, which is the Holy Spirit, whom the Father will send in my name, He shall teach you all things, and bring all things to your remembrance whatsoever I have said unto you."* Jesus spent a three-year span with them they had all of the tools necessary to carry out the ministry but one thing that is vitally important is the word that will be spoken in front of judges, the people, and other narrative nuisances. The Holy Spirit must give the wisdom and the understanding and the boldness to preach. It is not prevalent that when addressing preaching that we ask the question about scholastics and spirit. These concepts are normally divorced because we won't cross the gulf in practical theology that they are complimentary toward one another; and dare I say it's necessary for longevity in ministry. The days have long gone when you can abominably engage in fallacious free style preaching with the obscure objective to get people into their feelings. But the dangling danger to this is will it allow real people with real issues function in their frustrations and make formal decisions as to where their lives are headed.

Mining was hard work unbeknownst to some that left from their home in search for gold. It was stated that miners would have to mine on the surface through frigid water for 12 hours; others had to dig for 15 hours it was back breaking labor and most walked away with only a dollar worth of gold a day equivalent to 15 dollars today to care for their families. In this postmodern millennial era there is a mythical mirage that ministry is easy work or no work; that preaching doesn't come with pain; that ministering has no misery; and heralding is not harsh. The mining for masterpieces is back breaking labor. There are clergy that are known to have heart attacks; strokes; mental breakdowns; need psychological therapy; the fabric of their family life torn to the level of disrepair; late nights and early rises; questions of sufficiency; constant reading and reflection; restlessness because of the message; impromptu spiritual awakening to write a message at 3:00am; enormous attention given to their health; allowing life to pass them by not to mention the satanic attacks that are picking at any possible weakness in your armor. Preaching is back breaking labor. The question that follows is how is it bearable? It is through the relationship with the Holy Spirit because when you are called you are also kept. God gives unique joy to the preacher that the unqualified never experiences.

Unfortunately when mining ministers excavate there is always the possibility of injurious results; our calling as Paul Sharer articulated is to give "helpful hints for hurtful habits". This impeding danger while digging into a text can happen when we come across ancient material that appears to be adequate for homiletic usage but can become deadly because the information has not been verified and confirmed by scholars and practitioners of preaching. This can also happen while shopping in the bargain ben and the preacher purchases the books without sustaining proof of accuracy in the book. How can this be avoided? Through creating an acceptable purchase check list as follows: check the school of the author; the references in the back of the book; the publishing company; those who are forwarding the book do they have credible ethos? The ministering miner must prioritize disseminating information that is divinely inspired and not deadly to the spiritual infrastructure.

Underground mining is very tumultuous. It is known to reach 128 degrees and 100% humidity. During these conditions rocks can and do explode with spontaneity which has the force of a machine gun. The text that we lower ourselves into in the book of Hebrews reminds us it has tremendous force. Hebrews 4:12 renders *"For the word of God is alive and active sharper than any double-edged-sword it pierces even to dividing soul and spirit joints and marrow."* From these observations in mining there are conditions that are heated and harmful. It was known that miners would have to go take 30-minute breaks because of the heat. The mining of scripture can become heated as well, the fire of the glory of God can only be withstood for so long because of our anthropomorphistic nature therefore we must take breaks to digest and reflect on what God is communicating to us prior to us going back into the word of God.

There are so many that underestimate what it truly entails to be an effective miner for the eternal mysteries of God's word. There is a psychological toughness that has to be developed to keep your expectations God centered and elevate your own expectations over erroneous spectators. The preacher must be mentally strong from a domestic perspective; and an ecclesiastical perspective.

Black Powder

Black powder was used in mining originally. Black powder is modernly known as gunpowder. Gunpowder is the oldest of all explosives but the one thing about gunpowder compared to black powder is that you could not hide it. There would be a black cloud of smoke that would develop which was a sign of what you were using. (The World Book Encyclopedia Volume 5 1986,424) The effects of black powder should be similar to the effects of effective expository preaching. The effects of the spiritual should be obvious in the preaching presentation. We cannot call it preaching if the Spirit is not present; it is only a short talk or a motivational speech if we don't see the cloud of the Holy Spirit hovering over the herald as he preaches the unsearchable truths of scripture.

As mining became more sophisticated they relied on more efficient techniques in order to maximize their time that they spent mining. One of the concepts that would assist in the quickening of excavation was using black powder.

This was used as an explosive to access areas to potentially mine. This power allowed them to get to places they never could have arrived if they didn't have the black powder. As a miner of spiritual truth there are particular principles that you will not perceive in a pericope if you don't have the power of the Spirit. What makes the scriptures so fascinating is that in its inerrancy and inexhaustibility there are internal meaning that are waiting to be retrieved that God has placed deep in the text for us to find. Those miners that desire it must sojourn to dangerous places of spiritual warfare to receive it. I believe that there is an adversary that has a plan and also plots to disrupt and dissuade the preacher through egotism and people pleasing postures but we have to descend into warfare and ascend to heavenly thinking and plunge into prayer to ask God what is it that you desire for me to say and where should I say it. Adams advocated that "The preacher is concerned about people; that is why he is oriented toward what the Holy Spirit intends to do for them through preaching that passage." (Adams 1982,45)

Dynamite

With the increasing danger of using black powder there was another innovation of what they would use to remove massive piles of rocks and get into the inner bellies of the mountains to tap the gold supply so they used Dynamite. Dynamite was one of the most important industrial explosives used to blast out mines. (The World Book Encyclopedia Volume 5 1986,321) In antiquity, "Koine" Greek was a "common language" of the people in New Testament writings they had a word that reflects the expression of dynamite and that word is Dynamos. The word Dynamos in Greek Etymology is the word power. Which shows the explosiveness of the power of God to move things out of the promise peoples way or to place them onto God's agenda.

Miners need the Dynamos of the Spirit if the sermon is going to make effective moves. In homiletics the shifts in a text are called the movements of the text. Ministers that are mining for Masterpieces need to make use of the power that is available to them. There is a lot that a preacher has to get pass to gain the purest meaning possible to him or her. They must get beyond their embedded theology; they must get beyond the expectations of others; they must get beyond the spectating of congregational participation; they must get beyond their fleshly desire to be seen and heard and praised. Through the Spirit of God you can receive the power. Gardener Calvin Taylor stated in one of his marvelous messages on Job "when the window narrows that if you want power in your preaching God only has one way to give it to you trouble; pain; despair."

Eventually there was an infrastructure built underground to assistance and give bearable conditions for mining underground. Philip Deidesheimer created the calm stock roller. These methodology created by Deidesheimer allowed the structure to make it maneuverable and manageable to acquire the gold. As I think of the impact to the mining process that Philip Deidesheimer had, there was a greater impact for my homiletic thinking given by the Late Samuel Dewitt Proctor. Through his text the sound of the trumpet highlighting the massive importance of a proposition it has allow several clergy to create calm stocks underground to mining accurately the nuggets from the belly of the text. The proposition is the central meaning articulated in one to two sentences. It illumines the telos so that there is a guiding compass that is used as you are collecting nuggets from the text so that you will place them in the proper order so that what you offer the people from the mining ground is manageable and can be maneuvered. The Spirit I believe is a Spirit of order and I believe that the proposition gives us order because if the preacher is clueless as to where he or she is going then this creates cringing confusion throughout the congregation.

One thing that was the down side to Calm stock was that eventually these structures caused the death of fertility throughout the land. (Youtube Modern marvels) Massive areas of land were devastated and one of the main things that were killed were the trees. The issue that I have with any structure be it Proctors model of Proposition; Cradock's inductive preaching; Paul Scott Wilsons Four Pages; Marvin McMickle Sermonic Claim etc; is that when we adopt these techniques or methodologies and we begin going under ground in the text selfishly, we begin speaking a treeless gospel. When we go underground in the text to undermine God to destroy the tree and get rid of the tree so that we can have our golden moments in preacherdom—this becomes problematic. The miner never can come away with a masterpiece that transforms the compulsions of men and woman if he/she does not keep the tree at the nucleus of his or her preaching. This method of removal is what they call rapping the land. When you exclude the tree from the land of the text from mining it, this is considered rapping the text. The tree of Calvary that Jesus died on must be left as a reminder of why we preach in the first place. The hymnologist asked a pertinent question for every miner in the world, Should Jesus bear the cross alone and all men go free? No there's a cross for everyone there's a cross for you and a cross for me!

Now that you have the power lets peel back the next page and prepare for the next masterpiece!

Mining for Masterpieces

(Layer 2)

Practicing the Art of Preaching

Chapter 5

Mining Pan

There is always a Homiletic hope that resides in the preacher that the sermon will pan out. This hope must be met with your endorsement of the hard work demanded in Expository Preaching. Expository Preaching waits to leave its lasting treasures to those who are vested in the process though it may sometimes be daunting and demand more of your time; it eventually yields a robust result through textual accuracy.

The Puritans stated expository preaching builds a fire in the pulpit. Another advocate of expository preaching wrote; "Expository preaching gives the sound interpretation of a biblical text presenting the proper meaning of a passage in a logical unifying manner and showing its practicality." There have been countless arguments in the halls of homiletics concerning what is the best technique or style to escort and extract eternal biblical truths for external practical living. Craddock states "there is not a style of preaching, but it is just preaching." One ideology that I believe is undeniable is that Expository Preaching carries with it a dutiful imprint to declare what lies under the depths of a pericope. Since our focus in this text is Expository preaching we will need to be able to construct a working definition for preaching.

In the text *Preaching as Theology and Art* it states that "Christian preaching is above all else, the proclamation of the Word of God—the interpretation of biblical text for a listening congregation—and thereby the release of the powerful word of that text into the hearts and the minds."(Achtemeier 1984, 9) As I heard a professor say in the past, preaching is reaching. The question is reaching for what? Another preacher says aching is in the word too when it is not done correctly. There are so many who engage in preaching, but they have not prioritized reaching people for the purposes intended and that is a salvific response and servitude to the surrounding regions of humanity. I personally define preaching as blending revelation and reason to reassure and or call forth the righteous risk of faith in Jesus Christ. There are particular vehicles we lease to lead listeners on this journey

The vehicle that the present-day preacher uses to communicate is the sermon. The term sermon (which I mention in passing in the first section) in the Latin is sermo which means (speech). The term homiletics is the art and science of preaching. Homiletics derives from the term homila which we obtain the term homily. Homily is a short conversation. If we connect the dots preaching is a short spiritual conversation or speech.

Shaping the Sermon

To every sermon there is the origin of a journey. If the journey is going to be successful, oratorical objectives must be prioritized. This oratorical objective just simply means what is the sermon supposed to get done and can we see it prior to our arriving at the finish product. I remind you of my previous quote by Zig Ziglar, "you will never hit a target that you can't see." What can become more challenging is when you can't recognize or actualize what a target is. Paul Scherer once observed that "there are still some preachers who aim at nothing and who hit it squarely in the middle according to Wallace Fisher. (Fisher 1979, 73) O. C Edwards Jr. also observe: there are those who don't know what preaching should look like or sound like because they have not been around those who have precision to present to them viable paradigms. (Edwards 1982, 10)

One of the things that I have found to be useful for establishing a great base is the proposition. The proposition is a sermonic statement of stance. It is the one phrase or two sentences that you are willing to stand on and stand by throughout the period of proclamation. This statement will make you avoid rabbit trails that lead to mini loosely fit sermons that could cause confusion. This statement also helps you avoid the critique of James Stewart as those who preach skyscraper sermons putting one story upon another and never deal with the public text and convert it into a proclaimed text. Fred Craddock speaks of the typical result that some sermons are, that being "three sermonettes barely glued together". (Lowry 1985 15)

How do you construct this proposition? The first step is to identify what is making your homiletic vitals jump? What is burning in your heart? What has attracted you to this text? Is it a phrase, the crafting of the story or the position of the story? Was it the obscurity of the text? These are important questions you'll need to ask yourself; you'll also need to make a list, a written list. Don't try to hold this in your mind, you'll need to write the sermon notes and make it plain on tablets (paper or electronically)! It is important for us to get our ideas in front of us so do not be lazy in your learning as Jim Rohn says it. Write it down!

Once you have identified why you were lead to this text then begin to identify the theology of that particular prompting principle. Is the text dealing with Christology the doctrine of Christ; is it bathed in Pneumatology the doctrine of the Spirit or is it revealing Ecclesiology the doctrine of the Church. There will be a struggle to preach a biblical sermon if the proposition doesn't have strength in its theology, doctrine, apologetics, and proclamation. So that I don't make an egregious assumption that you know these terms, here is a concise meaning that we will return to later in this text.

Theology is a two-part word Theos (God) and logia (study or word about) which is the Study of God. Doctrine derives from the Latin word *doctrina*- the teaching and or instruction and *doctor*- the teacher. Christian truth and teaching passed on from generation to generation as the faith that was delivered to the saints.

Apologetics derives the Greek Etymology apologia "defense." (Encyclopedia of Early Christianity McHugh and Norris 1990, 65). Apologetics is Defined in Sermon without Ends as a theological/homiletical approach that uses the categories of knowledge thinking and values of the contemporary culture (Allen 3 2015). Proclamation in its Greek Etymology is kerygma, which focuses on the message. By having these three concepts covered it will help you to avoid heretical hutches for heralding and will aid you in creating a solid sermon structure.

Here is an example of a proposition from Luke 15:1-2

Now all the tax collectors and the sinners were coming near Him to listen to Him. Both the Pharisees and the scribes began to grumble, saying, "This man receives sinners and eats with them."

The main area or the *Sermonic Statement of Stance* is <u>This man receives sinners</u>.

Proposition: <u>*There is an incredible invitation that is extended beyond our injurious incidents*</u>

Here is the Break out: **Receives**—Incredible invitation; **Sinners**—Injurious Incidents

The key to a strong proposition is to make the language sensitive to the contemporary audience. To do so you must make sure it is true to the meaning of the ancient text. When this is done properly you have in your sermonic statement of stance biblical integrity and blaring interest from congregants. This gives you an opportunity to create a masterpiece.

Mull your work over and be sure that you don't just accept the first proposition that is drafted when the proposition is completed. You must be sure! Challenge yourself to create two to three propositions, this is important because we do not want to just have a proposition we should have the best proposition. By all means, do not scrap the rest, that is—the leftover propositions. They could lead to the creating of another sermon or could possibly become a phrase that could reiterate the point you are making in another area of the sermon. It could actually become a point or a leading sentence in your introduction.

There are those who are not fans of the deductive form of preaching and then there are those persons who are disciples of Fred Craddock who prefer the inductive style of preaching (referring to the proposition as a water ring at the bottom of a boiling pot). If you have an inductive style of preaching you don't want to give your sermonic statement of stance immediately. You'll want to delay your purpose of proclamation until the end. This means that you need to tie your thoughts to what will contemporarily draw the interest of the listener and work your way to the gospel meaning. From an inductive viewpoint pick a topic:

Telling Topic: Hurting people need to be received

Theology: The church needs to be open to the realization of these wounds

Mission: We have been called by God to be an Oasis to the Least, the Lost and the Left out

After you have addressed these three areas you can then work on the sermon that you are intrigued to preach. Whatever style you are attempting to preach, there is a must to chart your course and remain on that course so that the shape of your sermon is a silhouette of what the intent was from the outset of the sermonic statement of stance.

Theological Approach of the Text

Initial theology

As you start the homiletic journey there is a theology that is already programmed within your mind prior to beginning your research. This theology is your first theology or what I would like to call the initial theology. Your initial theology is the sum of your embedded theology, your presumptions, assumptions, the stories and strategies that have been stuffed deep in the back of your mind over the years. It is what you were raised to believe to be true and because we've gathered so many of these principles/theologies during our lifetime when we encounter biblical genres we tend to revert back into those familiar belief systems.

These theological thoughts breed the areas of conceptual comfort. These thoughts allow for us to immediately get the sermonic task over. We don't like our thoughts challenged or having to ponder over other possibilities because we already have enough on our calendars. For many we have office secretaries, Siri, or Alexa reminding us that we already have jammed packed schedules so why spend the extra time refining and retooling our thoughts. Les Brown spoke of a book that stated what if you wake up one morning at the end of life just to discover you had it wrong what then? As we take time to interpret scripture do we take the time to make sure that our thinking is not biblical errant? This demands the moving of one's pride out of the way.

Once I conversed with a friend and they were instructing a class in Theology. The class was exciting and educational but the bump in the road came when ethnic differences from the contemporary and antiquity were addressed and viewed as not being relational. He told me how the student became aggressive and disrespectful even borderline belligerent all because their first theology was challenged. Many who have their initial theology challenged either shutdown or become very argumentative, attacking the person that has the nerve to change the narrative of their theology or do what my mentor Abraham Smith says, "attempting to trim their growing edges". If we can't be challenged in our first theology our closed-minded disposition will have us shelve spiritual truth that you will never enjoy because you will expire prior to the enjoyment date.

Refine theology

Those clergy or miners that are open to accuracy will venture into a deliberative theology. During the mining process there was an invention that was called a shaker that separated the gold from the other elements and this is what refine theology does in sermon preparation. This step happens after you have done the research and you have confirmed your findings it can totally change your thinking concerning a doctrinal issue or it can reaffirm what you have already thought about God. The preachers that take their time and treat the sermon as an oven process as opposed to the microwave process are able to enjoy what is delivered from the heat of the process. Using the oven process it may seem timely but it's thorough from beginning to end; the right questions have been asked, the manuscript has had time to marinade a day or two and you can come back and pick it up to see if it is done, and if you still agree after a day of theological reflection. With the microwave process, it may be hot to the touch, but it can be cold to the taste. In other words, it's lukewarm. In the book of Revelation, it apprises us about how God feels about a lukewarm church, which I believe, is God's view of a lukewarm sermon as well. If only more clergy took the time to engage in the oven process, many heretical and apostate statements would have never seen the light of day.

Whatever we are going to give to the people should be profitable. 2 Tim 3:16 NASB *All Scripture is inspired by God and profitable for teaching, for reproof, for correction, for training in righteousness; so that the man of God may be adequate, equipped for every good work.*

There was an experiment that was held which demanded that a man eat MacDonald's for 30 straight days without eating anything else. After the 30 days were completed they put a home cook meal on one side of him: a steak, mash potatoes, string beans and ice-cold water. On the other side a Big Mac and Fries and a Coca-Cola. The man's male nourished hand was shaking as he reached toward the Big Mac and Fries. This experiment's results I believe reveals the new normal for those in ecclesiastical theological circles today. Contemporarily preachers have raised a generation on processed spiritual meat in the pulpit and it lacks profitability for spiritual wholeness and progressive purity. There are those who have not compromised to serve such a damaging doctrinal diet and they come to some churches as ecclesiastical stomach pumpers so as to purify parishioner's theology of all of the cross contamination that has transpired.

Prior to writing a complete sermon, there must be a serious yet strategic observation of what this sermon will accomplish within them. I've found objectives in sermons to be helpful and an advocate for the utilization of them in your preparation. I also encourage you to write out what you seek to accomplish through your message.

Sermonic objectives

1.

2.

3.

    The aim of the sermon should be to find the telos, the purpose of the sermon. After the telos has been defined then scan your proposition to make sure that it properly lines up with the biblical truths that you are about to proclaim. Now that we've established the direction of the sermon and how it will pan out, now that we can identify the mining pockets this will help us create an expository sermon that will help move people's lives from misery to a masterpiece. If you are ready to be lowered into the next mining cage for gold, jump in and continue digging because you'll find that there is gold down there!

Chapter 6

Mining Pockets

Thomas Liske in his text *Effective Preaching* makes the case that "unfortunately the greatest single weakness of the average sermon is the weakness of diagnosis". (Liske 1960, 37.) There is a lack of attentiveness to what the sermon should do, what it should address and why should it be spoken in the season that we are currently in or entering. "The committed preachers, the faithful servants of God— do not neglect their tools". (Achtemeier 1980, 22)

Research is one of the most underestimated steps in sermonic preparation. There are preachers that are yearning to construct expository sermons, but they don't have enough scholarly information to sustain this style of preaching. This problematic famine of available resources to the preacher produces a textual or topical sermon on steroids, which are cluttered with charismatic clichés.

This pointed precision in the time of study reminds me of the packaging, which was done for my carryout order from the restaurant

Apple Bee's. As I examined the contents I saw a check for accuracy sticker with the name of the person that checked the order. This small sticker was an indicator that a thorough inspection was implemented with specific detail to ensure that what had been ordered matched the contents in the carryout container. As each preacher reads the text we must do our research. This research becomes a sticker that the sermon has been checked for accuracy. One of the worst things to discover is that what is on the menu of the Bible fails to match the material found within the sermon. Every sermon we proclaim has our signature on it and we are accountable to God for what was left out or what was put in that was not authorized. In order for us to avoid this costly mistake, we need to be aware of the biblical story.

Knowing the Bible

One area that is grossly neglected in expository preaching is the demand for preachers to know the scriptures thoroughly. This ideology is supported when the scholar affirmed "No preacher can proclaim the word persuasively unless he or she knows God's story in depth and experiences His love firsthand that will not let go" (Lowry 1985, 70). There are several preachers who are not avid Bible readers; they do not read the Bible daily which causes a great delay in their ability to make the necessary connections confirming the first law of mention, which enables them to also connect with other books contextually synchronizing them in a way that will crystallize the textual meaning for congregant's consumption. The one basis of our authority is the Holy Scriptures. If we do not preach out of them, we should not be preaching at all. (Achtemeier 1980, 16) There are some preachers that have never read the entire Bible through, not even one time! The possible reason for this unfortunate reality is because there hasn't been a model feasible and friendly enough to the preacher that'll allow them to fulfill such a task.

After taking some time to reflect over this challenge, I had an "ah ha" moment in my office and came up with the rule of 4. The rule of 4 is committing to read 4 chapters of the Bible each day, seven days a week which will result in your reading 28 chapters a week. This pattern should be kept even if the chapters are long or if the chapters are short. The entire point of this exercise is to remain consistent. I know that there are many preachers saying I can do much more than that. My response to that is, you may be right but are you consistently doing it daily? If you read 4 chapters a day it is easier to focus your attention on the stories and to remember the important parts to the story. If this method of study is implemented, then you will be able to read through the Bible in a year or shorter. The rule of 4 will help with your scriptural recall and will benefit you when mining the ground for nuggets in expository preaching.

Expository Examples

The next step requires that you collect sermons and or outlines that have mastered the Expository preaching style. The structure of an expository sermon needs to become visible to you. Raymond Bailey's suggestions pick up on the importance of the oral thought patterns in the texts. This will also allow you to see the way in which their personality and gifting allows them to approach the text in a different way. Another format that you can use is the digital recorded format. Take the time to listen to a sermon that is in the style of expository preaching. These expository sermons can be found on Facebook, YouTube, and or Periscope. The first couple of times just listen. Listen for the rhythm, for the transitions, for the movements, the mixture of scriptures and other materials that have been weaved into the sermon. This will help train your ear so that when you are listening to yourself you'll be able to determine if the structure sounds similar. Initially, do not worry about the content.

Just as a musician can be trained by ear the preacher was originally trained by ear. During the times in antiquity there was a focus on oral tradition because everything was not in print. This was why God told Moses to tell Joshua in Joshua 1 to meditate on his word day and night. It is also cited historically that Augustine was displeased when visiting Ambrose for not reading the Scriptures aloud because there was great significance in the oratorical nature of speaking God's word. Reading and sound went together. (Brilioth 1965, 43) The same is true about hearing expository preaching. It allows for you to be empowered by the audible utterance that unfolds the message and eventually can move you toward the method. We must remember that the word according to Brilioth, uttered actually equals outer. When we are to utter the things of God there is a need for an outer expression that should come forth.

After you have taken the time to listen to the sermon the next step is your need to take copious notes while listening to the preacher. You need to try to construct and extract the skeleton from the sermon that you've heard. When you have mastered this you now partly understand the shaping of the sermon and its structure, which can assist you in shaping your own crafted expository sermon. In the same way, until you have a working understanding and are following this format remain attentive and observant until you can confidently interject innovation as you are shaping your very own.

Sermonic Weaving

The research in which you are engaging in is what I call in my theological training school, *Seminary on Wheels*, sermonic weaving. This is the process of when you take from the different books, journals, commentaries, and lectures and weave them together so that you may have the finish product. These are working ideas, revelation and reason that will yield their weight in gold as you walk through the sermonic creative process. When you mine gold you dig up everything together but then you must implement a purging process. This is where you may separate the impurities that may be found among the gold. The materials you've dug up must be sent through the fire so that the good can be extracted from the bad. The gold then goes through the molding process to be prepped properly for presentation under the jeweler's glass. Everything the preacher researches should not come to the pulpit. But, that which is selected must be taken through the weaving process.

Doing so will allow you to eliminate the impurities before drafting that particular sermon. It will reveal what must be burnt off so that the finish product may be presented before sub specie aeternitatis, under the light of eternity.

Figure 1.1

Sermonic Weaving Sample

Tools for Expository Preaching

Character Study

|

Manner and Cus. — \ | /— **Ancient Writings**

Literary—*<u>Sermon</u>*—**Historical**

Bible Dict.—/ | \ —**Biblical Text**

/ | \

Illustration Etymology Journal Articles

Commentaries

Preachers beware of Commentaries! This statement for some may evoke emotions that scream, "I told you so! They are unnecessary!" Others may be thinking, "This young man has no clue about the bounty that comes from these books." Well this statement was made with the intent to advise you that we don't shape our sermons based on the totality of what the commentary has stated. There are some preachers that have mishandled commentaries much like those who mishandle prescriptions. They take too much and endanger themselves with a possible theological overdose.

The commentary should not be consulted initially because you don't want to cause suicide to your original thought in a sermon. Creativity is the fashioning of a sermon into such an artistic and effective whole that the Word of God spoken through the text is allowed to create that reality of which it speaks. (Achtemeier 1980, 12)

Journal Articles

The Journal articles are another beneficial source that is available to enhance preachers sermonic weaving. These journals are mostly created from the writings that were produced when there was a call for papers for an association for theological advancement, be it the (AOH) Academy of Homiletics or the (SBL) Society of Biblical Literature etc. These are important because this can inform you concerning the new trends that are developing regarding theological challenges in the church and in the academic setting. Reading these journal entries will give you a command on the relevance of contemporary theological questions or doctrinal issues. This will provide a relevant and fresh academic understanding concerning the selected text.

Magazine Articles

There are Preaching Magazines that take out time to examine text. You will be very fortunate to find biblical scholars of all walks of life that take time to give their contribution toward a designated scripture or subject matter. These magazines will give you a concise informative read on historical findings or comparative views of the commentators that will cause us to choose a course of action from the magazine articles themselves. This allows you to fill the homiletic holes in with information that is laity friendly and academically strong.

These are just a couple of resources that one can use to begin to weave together. There are different Commentaries, Background Commentaries, Bibles and other tools useful for utilization to strengthen what is uttered in an unfamiliar fashion and to familiarize them with the God of the scriptures. Please refer to the references of this text in order to further your research through resources when venturing into unfamiliar territory. It may possibly lead to a gold mine.

Introduction to the Bible

Those who desire an in-depth view of the scriptures that they are seeking to excavate from should look at the chiastic structure and author's intent. Also, the audience will benefit immensely when they use an introduction to the Bible. To explore even further, exposing one's self to single books by authors designated to that book will give an unprecedented viewpoint to the interpreter to sharpen the interpretation.

Research, Research and more Research will yield to you the homiletic accuracy that is necessary to create sermons that are superiorly shaped and weaved with worthwhile notes that will make the listener say it was worth their time to hear the word from your homiletic perspective.

Chapter 7

Mining the Parts

It only takes one idea, or one thought in order to spring you toward the mining fields of the text and to place you on the trail to uncovering a masterpiece. There is so much power and potential in a sermon idea that is ready to be blossomed into an effective form of expository preaching which will expose the people to confirmation and affirmation. Fred Craddock suggests; "any experienced preacher knows what it is like to get an idea. It usually comes suddenly and unexpectedly but there is a vivid impression that this is it, that we have struck pay dirt". (Craddock 1981, 22-23)

The structure that is presented in these outlines and figures should not make you succumb to being enslaved by the manuscript but it should only offer help in the shaping of the sermon as a system of support. The structure of the sermon is the pictorial of a grocery cart. No one stops and says to fellow shoppers did you see the outstanding grocery carts? Absolutely not! These grocery carts have one job and that is to hold the contents you desire to purchase and transported from the shelves to the register and then to your automobile. The structure that we use should not be praised but how the structure allowed the passage to be portable enough to get the pericope(s) contents to my home and my heart. Further in this chapter focus will be given to the essential nuts and bolts of the sermon so that we can afford some connectivity in the ideas and so that the sermon can be understood and made practical for ministry and daily living for those among the pew. This chapter will also explore the parts of the expository sermon while defining them and demonstrating the importance of each component to the sermon building process.

Figure 1.2 Romans 12

Here is S Model (Skeletal Model) for Expository Preaching

Skeletal Model

Proposition—Sincerity of sacrifice leads to stellar service
Thesis-Your work is a wonderful expression of your appreciation for God
Antithesis—Obligation opposed to an open heart to serve

I. Virtuously Vested Interest

A. Intimacy

B. Invitation

C. Inclusive

II. Victorious Venture(s)

A. Member

B. Mercy

C. Matchless

III. Vigorous Viewing

A. Sacrificial

B. Sacred

C. Service

Sermonic Conclusion

Figure 1.3

Here we will explore the M (Meaty) Model

Meaty Model

Proposition—Sincerity of sacrifice leads to stellar service

Thesis-Your work is a wonderful expression of your appreciation for God

Antithesis—Obligation opposed to an open heart to serve

Synthesis: Move from the obstacle of obligation to an opulent opportunity to serve

Raise Question: How do I press while I'm dealing with the pressure?

I. Virtuously Vested Interest: Paul gives a personal plea when he formally had a persistent persecution.

A. Intimacy—Paul gives here a specific address

B. Invitation—Paul gives here a special address

C. Inclusive—Paul gives a spacious address (There is room for others)

II. Victorious Venture(s)—The brethren are the catalyst of Christ for world change

A. Member—Believers are classified

B. Mercy—Bondage has been canceled

C. Matchless – Blessing of the Creator

III. Vigorous Viewing—The sacrificial system must move from dead to living

A. Sacrificial—Evidence of my Participation

B. Sacred—No Evil through my Participation

C. Service—Eagerness in my Participation

Figure 1.4 Romans 12

Here is the F (Functioning) Model

Functioning Model

Introduction—Good service is just hard to find; various businesses, restaurants and other organizations. These businesses appear to always have help wanted signs placed in the window, it is probably due to the fact that not only is good service hard to find, but good people that possess a strong work ethic are also hard to find.

Proposition—Sincerity of sacrifice leads to stellar service. (This is the reason for my preaching presentation today, because we need sacrificial service in society for the Sovereign)

Thesis-Your work is a wonderful expression of your appreciation for God. (How do we show God our Appreciation? Use a comparison of how those in the bible gave their appreciation.)

Antithesis—Obligation as opposed to an open heart to serve. (How do individuals have rebellious hearts concerning their service?)

Synthesis: Move from the obstacle of obligation to an opulent opportunity to serve

Raise Question: How do I press while I'm dealing with the pressure?

I. Virtuously Vested Interest: Paul gives a personal plea when he formally had a persistent persecution.

A. Intimacy—Paul gives here a specific address—Paul places a personal emphasis

B. Invitation—Paul gives here a special address—Paul invites those in Christ

C. Inclusive—Paul gives here a spacious address (There is room)— Those of us that desire to follow Christ we are included as well. There is room at the cross for you! (ending song for this point)

II. Victorious Venture(s)—The brethren are the catalyst of Christ for world change

A. Member—Believers are classified—Paul is specific about his charge to the church

B. Mercy—Bondage has been canceled—Paul mentions how they are making the mission it is his mercy. Unmerited Favor

C. Matchless – Blessings of the Creator—Paul verifies the provisions that comes from God

III. Vigorous Viewing—The sacrificial system must move from deadened to living

A. Sacrificial—Evidence of my participation—The Sacrifice is dying and living at the same time

B. Sacred—No Evil through my participation—The holiness that God requires for you to serve him with sincerity and truthfully

C. Service—Eagerness in my participation—Those that were in the church then and right now are expected to give real ministry through service.

Sermonic Conclusion

Exegetical Concepts and their Importance

Proposition—This particular concept is vital because it is the core of the sermon. The life and breath or meaningful movement of the sermon derives from this concept. The proposition has been referred to as the Sermonic Claim; Major Concern of the Text; Big idea; Main Objective.

Proposition view from the Text—In Romans 12 we are connecting sacrifice and service as being the words to withdraw for our proposition. This allows for us to develop a target and a vein that we are going to commit ourselves to.

Thesis—The Thesis statement is the main idea of a text. It is a statement of what you desire to speak about. This statement is developed after you find the core of the sermon in the proposition.

Thesis Function—As we craft the sermon, the Thesis plays a major role in the introduction. The thesis is expressed through stories; profound questions; and/or experiences that bring the sermon to life.

Antithesis—The Antithesis is the polar opposite of whatever the thesis may be. The proposition is a pivotal concept to this as well. We can select the antithesis for introductory purposes.

Antithesis Function—The Antithesis may be used from the very start of the introduction or it may be in the shift from Thesis to Antithesis. The Antithesis will be used during the sermonic shifts or the movements of the text, which creates tension that draws interest from the listener.

Synthesis—This is the transitory concept it begins to move you from the introduction to the body of the sermon. This must be connected well or you can loss the listener.

Raise Question—The Raise Question is really important because it is a question that could be looming in the minds of the listeners. This question also gives a relative ease to go into the first movement of the sermon.

Sermonic Shifts—This area of the text is often referred to as the "main points" and many have also recently begun referring to them as "movements". These shifts should hammer home the proposition. It supports the sermonic claim and gives validity to the reason for the presence and operative function of a proposition. A movement is of fundamental importance not simply because the speaker wants to get somewhere in his presentation but because the movement itself is to be an experience of the community in sharing the word. (Craddock 1981, 54)

Etching the Right Ethics in Expository Preaching

Vocabulary

If you have not already realized it, let me inform you that there is a need for a working vocabulary to become an effective expository preacher. When you are attempting to create sub points the need for word variety that explains it in antiquity and is yet understandable in the contemporary is a tedious task for even the most experienced exegete. The student of Expository preaching will do themselves a great service by learning a word daily from the secular and biblical dictionary or lexicon so that you can extemporaneously create points prior to you retreating to the dictionary. This working vocabulary will allow you to create a chemistry in studying that freely allows creativity to flow in the moment.

Filing System

The filing system is invaluable to the expositor's experience. This is established through the process of devotional readings that I spoke of earlier (Reading 4 chapters a day). Taking notes of profound statements and filing them in alphabetical order or under a particular category will lend itself useful as well when it is time to create the connections in the movements of the sermon.

Biblical Theology

The power of biblical exegesis should not be underestimated in this process. This is one of the most important parts of expository preaching. Expository Preaching prides itself above all as being Biblical Preaching! The exegete must know how will all of these parts in scripture come together which will speak forth a principle that is practical and clear for the listener. Good theology will lead to good expository preaching, while poor theology will expose poor expository preaching.

Thinking Expository

Never underestimate the power of thinking in this process. Too many preachers come to this textual process too light hearted and they miss the hours of labor in thinking that must transpire to create a sermon that is textually true and practically illuminating. Rev. James T. Cleveland was correct when he stated; "if there is a mist in the pulpit, there's a fog in the pew". There are countless hours that are surrendered to bring together each set of materials and align them in a way that maintains the direction of the sermon and fulfills the divine task of the telos of the passage of the scriptures.

Chapter 8

Mining Purification

During the mining process, purification is paramount to yield dimensional desirables. As I alluded to earlier there is a purification process that is necessary for doctrinally solid and theologically sound expository preaching. In preaching unfortunately there are sometimes illegitimate licensing used to form erroneous interpretations. According to Ronald Allen, "In the Expository Sermon the presence of the biblical text tends to remind the preacher to ground the sermon in a theological point of view." (Allen 1992, 7) This forms an escapism from ego being implemented in the expressed perspective of the text.

There is one area that I believe can assist the preacher tremendously in the purification process and that is Detailed Analysis. This is the bodyguard of the text that protects against theological ruffians who will attempt to bogart their dogmatic disposition onto the text and upon those who are orally taking it in. The Detailed Analysis is where we are able to engage in our detective or journalism work. The question that I am asked frequently is how do we differentiate the importance of the details that we are examining.

The answer to which details you should focus on is based upon two areas: the telos (the goal and or purpose of the text) and the proposition of the sermon that is being used to shape the sermon. It is in the detailed analysis that you come across the necessary queries of the text; the Who, What, When, Where, How, and Why. Lets take a moment to reveal each question's substantiation to the process.

Who

The "who" deals with the nouns, pronouns, or proper nouns of the text. This gives us a glimpse of how the event transpired from the eyes of the characters in the text, be it major or minor characters. One caution; do not be too imaginative, this can lead to eisegesis. The question who, describes who is important; who has brought this problem about; who activated a decision; Who needs the help; Who was found in the sin; Who made the move. This question "who", allows you to quickly find who are the antagonist (villian) and the protagonist (hero) or who is in collaboration. As you discover who these individuals are it will lead you to character studies. I advise in your spare time that you invest time in doing character studies. It will help further expose a better exegetical reenactment of the text.

What

Stories are generally channels of communication that allow for us to find out what happens. The verbs really own this question. Because it is an action that has already been taken or will be taken in the future predicated upon another action.

The question here is, what happen? They came together; They believed; They fell by the wayside; He called even louder; They tore up the roof; He washed his hands; Jesus Wept; This question is a store house for all of the action. Most of your main points will derive from what has transpired in the text. This question really yields to you movements and pivots in the passage that gives a point of reference of how we should engage ourselves accordingly if you use the deductive formatting.

When

Time is a virtue for this specific area. Time is used in the scriptures to create the scene. Chronos referring to abstract notion of time in general as well as a span or interval of time and Kairos often has connotations of the appropriate or decisive moment or period of time. (Morisada Reitz Henry NIDB Volume 5 2009, 598) There is a distinctive meaning behind the time given in scripture. Isaiah 6; it was in the year King Uzziah died I saw the Lord. Luke 1:5 In the days of Herod, king of Judea, there was a priest named Zacharias, of the division of Abijah; this was a setup to introduce John the Baptist. This word "when" also is a word of predication; When you do this then he will do that!

Where

What is the location where it happened? Places have names which are very significant; we have the Mountain in Genesis 22 where Abraham named it "the Lord will provide" and what about Jacob in Genesis 32 where he wrestles and he calls it "I seen God face to face and remained alive". How about John 5 the place where the paralytic man was impeded in his impotence but the place was known for "mercy".

These names are significant but there needs to be a contextualizing of those names so that there is no contaminated creation of awkward assessments of the text.

How

How do we get there is the functioning of this word. The "how" in the sermon is what my Pastor calls the "Marching Orders of the Sermon". The how question opens us up to "how do we get it done or accomplished?" This is the pronouncement of practicality. If there is no leading of the congregant on the journey to accomplish anything then this becomes a waste of time for the congregation. This can also become a pathetic display of disregard for the equipping and ignition of kingdom ministry.

Why

This question lands us on the runway of reasoning. If we don't have a reason most people won't bother to listen or engage the sermon. Professor Edward Branch used to say it doesn't matter how many points you have one or even five just make sure that after you've completed the sermon you're sure you've had a point for preaching it. This question makes us ask the crucial question why should I follow the plan? Why should I take all of the steps? This is the punch line of the sermon, so to speak. If there is no punch line we get caught in the inertia of the sermon and it carries us into unauthorized areas that don't belong in the sermon. In the Elements of Biblical Exegesis Gorman quotes John Chrysostom on the importance of Detailed Analysis when he suggest:

"It is not in the interest of extravagant ambition that we trouble ourselves with this detailed exposition, but we hope through such painstaking interpretation to train you in the importance of not passing over even one slight word or syllable in the Sacred

Scriptures. For they are not ordinary utterances, but the very expression of the Holy Spirit, and for this reason it is possible to find great treasure even in a single syllable."(Gorman 2009, 101)

Detailed Analysis should focus on the following:

Repetition in the Text: What word repeatedly arises in the narrative and is there a name that they are connected to or a land?

Etymology Studies: There are so many preachers that give biblical languages a bad reputation but I believe that languages help to expose the inner workings of a word helping to provide clarity. Biblical Languages carry bruises when the individuals hearken their (languages) presence to hail themselves as a homiletic herculean expositor. The languages are only an entrance to get you into the room of understanding.

Themes: There are themes that the author uses in the book to inform the reader of the significance of particular traditions, theologies, teachings, and influences that are permeating in its textual construct. When you read any book of the Bible it would be wise not to miss the trees for the forest because they make up the forest.

Comparison and Contrast: There are list and different areas in the scriptures that desire to reveal who are deemed as the righteous and those who are deemed as unrighteous. This rhetoric is used to give a clear understanding and distinction. There should be no ambiguity that can lead to the abandoning of righteousness or appropriate behavior. The writer uses the syntax of lining these actions or characteristics up so that those readers can make conscious decisions.

Lessons through Stories: The details of one story sometimes in biblical narrative can give insight to an episodic encounter that is directly next door to it. Mark uses this method quite frequently. If you pay close attention the actions of the previous story is what helps illumine the present story.

These are a few things that you need to take your time and examine when searching out biblical truth in expository preaching. To avoid having to pick from sermonic straws, it is very important in Expository preaching that you exercise three steps: Interpretation, Connection and Explanation.

Three Step Rule for Expository Preaching

Interpretation

Hermeneutics is a vital part to expository preaching. Using the focused theological lens to carefully select areas of the text for further investigation is necessary. After you have those words or phrases in mind engage in exegesis from the proclaimed text and expose the meanings that lay beneath the surface or on the surface.

Connection

What Scriptures are contextually accurate to place within this sermon? The connections must be proper from a customary perspective and they must be accurate from a cultural point of view as well. Be aware that just because scriptures have similar words it does not mean that they have the same meaning. Connections must be confirmed based on the principle that has already been established from the beginning. If there is no confirmation don't make the connection; the scripture should assist in explaining scripture. The connection should not birth confusion or abruptly removing us from our homiletic sermon mapping in the creative imagery of Ronald Allen's homiletic language.

Explanation

Expository within the very nature of its syllogism reveals what its task is, and that is to expose. The sermon should cautiously and carefully expose what the text means. This exposure allows for the opportunity to be the barter for people to follow what has been revealed or to reject it. This explanation is the first cousin to revelation. In the expository preaching process there should be revelation of what we didn't see before even though it was there in plain sight. I believe there is an insightfulness that belongs to those who are spiritually connected to God to see and understand things that pertain to the kingdom of God within the preaching moment.

Those that are serious about the exegetical process will go to great lengths to discover the nuggets that are under the foreign soil of the text. It certainly takes a special hunger and irrevocable tenacity to continue digging when a mining minister comes up empty. Even though there are challenges and even experiences threatening heretical misgivings that are attractive, with raw hands and a tattered homiletic covering we dig for divine truth so that the listeners can receive a word that has been picked, processed and purified for public proclamation.

I believe there is Gold in those Homiletic Hills and pray that by this time you believe this as well. Keep digging and searching,

I believe you will hit the mother load of biblical truths after while. Picks down, shovels down, and knees down . . . lets pray!

Miners Prayer

Lord I thank you for these mining ministers. Please give them the strength to keep digging through discouragements and through disappointments. When they are clutched by the spirit of never mind or complacency please drop a nugget to keep them pursuing the godly gold that will forever change our lives and their lives on this journey . . . In the Name of the Greatest Preacher of all time, in Jesus' Name Amen!

Common Questions of Expository Preaching

There are so many questions that preachers have concerning the structure, strategy and strength of Expository Preaching. In this section of the book I have designated an area to answer frequent asked questions hoping that it will lead the preacher on a progressive track to become a better expositor.

Question 1: Where do I start in the process of writing more Expository Sermons?

Answer 1: The best way that I have discovered in strengthening your execution of writing strong Expository sermons is to attempt to master the textual sermon structure. The textual sermon normally has 1 to 5 verses. The outline in the textual format is similar to the expository preaching format with the exception of sub telos that form throughout each movement. The movement section of the sermon is a vital part. Gathering the superior contents and shaping them in a clear cognitive pattern which causes challenge and conscious steps toward life improvement will set your pace to become a better expositor.

Question 2: Expository versus Exposition?

Answer 2: These two concepts are easily confused because the homiletic structural elements are the same. The difference between the two is the expository sermon is used as a means of persuasion in preaching. The Exposition focuses is on provoking thinking in a crowd but may not lead to a decision. Exposition is really the lane of the lecturer more than the lane of the preacher.

Question 3: What's the hardest part of creating an Expository Sermon?

Answer 3: I believe the hardest part is maintaining the connections of the expository sermon that should keep its alignment with the main principle and telos of the text. These connections must have their context thoroughly checked to ensure that you don't take a scripture and bend it for the purposes of the sermon when it is battered in the context of the original scripture.

Question 4: Are there any differences in African American Expository Preaching and Eurocentric Evangelical Expository Preaching?

Answer 4: I believe there is a difference because the lens in which we preach from has totally different filters. The aim of the preacher is very different in their respective cultures. In the African American Context there is a lengthy history of bondage physiologically and psychologically. These areas of bondage must be acknowledged and spoken to while also keeping the integrity of the text, all the while connecting other scriptures in context and preaching Jesus. In some Eurocentric Evangelical content, expository preaching there is no need to deal with that type of suffering because it would be futile to frequent this subject seeing that some of the audiences have not experienced those injustices.

In addition, another difference I believe in the two preachers is the European Expository sermon has more simplicity but yet has profundity in its construct while the African American has acrobatic elements which vouches for the creativity and style in the story of African American preaching. Of course this assessment is not true in every circumstance because there are charismatic Eurocentric styles of preaching as well; but a broad view of this activity has been my experience as well as found in much of my readings in my short tenure in homiletics.

Question 5: Are there cons or draw backs to Expository preaching?

Answer 5: When a congregation is malnourished in the area of preaching or biblical knowledge, Expository preaching will be great because it gives a wider view of scripture but also can become challenging because of the possibility of suffocating them with too much information. The Expository method Exposes them but the draw back is when there is such a gravity of the lack of Exposure it puts people in scriptural culture shock because they aren't accustomed to receiving that level of impartation from the pulpit.

Question 6: When is Expository Preaching most beneficial?

Answer 6: Expository Preaching is most needed when a person is engaged in preaching a series. This method allows for you to take the same scriptures and expand on them in new and enlightening ways. This type of preaching gives the space to expand and contract in a preaching presentation without stripping the scriptures of its strengths.

References

Adams, Jay E. 1982. Preaching with Purpose. Phillipsburg, New Jersey: Presbyterian and Reformed Publishing Company.

Achtemeier, Elizabeth R. 1980. Creative Preaching. Nashville, TN: Abingdon Press

Achtemeier, Elizabeth R. 1984. Preaching As Theology & Art. Nashville, TN: Abingdon Press

Allen, Ronald J. 1992. Preaching The Topical Sermon. Louisville, Kentucky: Westminster/John Knox Press.

Allen, Ronald J. and Allen, Wesley O. 2015. The Sermon without End. Nashville TN: Abingdon Press

Brilioth, Yngve. 1965. A Brief History of Preaching. Philadelphia: Fortress Press.

Cahill, Dennis M. 2007. The Shape of Preaching. Grand Rapids, MI: Baker Books.

Craddock Fred B. 1981. As One without Authority. Nashville, TN : Abingdon.

_____. 2011. Craddock On The Craft OF Preaching. St. Louis, Missouri: Chalice Press.

Duvall, Hays J. and Duvall, Scott J. 2012. Grasping God's Word. Grand Rapids, MI: Zondervan.

Edwards, O.C. 1982. Elements of Homiletic. Collegeville Minnesota: The Liturgical Press.

Eslinger, Richard L. 1996. Pitfalls in Preaching. Grand Rapids, MI : William B. Eerdmans Publishing Company.

Fee, Gordon and Stuart, Douglas 2003. How to Read the Bible for All Its Worth, Grand Rapids MI. : Zondervan

Finley, James. 1986. Wake Up and Preach! New York: Alba House.

Foster, Richard J. 1998. Celebration of Discipline. New York NY: HarperCollins.

Ferguson, Everett. 1990. Encyclopedia of Early Christianity. New York: Garland Publishing.

Gibbs, A.P. 2002. The Preacher and His Preaching. Kansas City: Walterick Publishers.

Gorman, Michael J. 2009. Elements of Biblical Exegesis. Peabody Massachusetts: Hendrickson Publishers.

Heisler, Greg. 2007. Spirit—LED Preaching. Nashville, TN : B&H Academic.

Koller, Charles W. 1964. How to Preach Without Notes. Grand Rapids, MI: Baker Books.

Long, Thomas. 1985. Preaching And The Literary Forms of the Bible. Philadelp: Fortress Press.

Lewis, Gregg and Ralph Lewis L. 1983. Inductive Preaching Helping People Listen. Wheaton Illinois: Cross Ways Books.

Lischer, Richard. 1987. Theories of Preaching. Durham, North Carolina: The Labyrinth Press.

Liske, Thomas. 1960. Effective Preaching. New York: The Macmillian Company.

Lowry, Eugene. 1985. Doing Time in the Pulpit. Nashville TN: Abingdon Press.

Macleod, Ronald. 1987. The Problem of Preaching. Philadelphia: Fortress Press.

Phillip, Joseph. 1989. The Joy of Preaching. Grand Rapids MI: Kregrel Publications.

Rhondes, Ron. 2005. Christian Denominations. Eugene, Oregon:Harvest House Publisher.

Robinson, Haddon W. 2001. Biblical Preaching. Grand Rapids, MI: Baker Academic.

Rueter, Alvin C. 1997. Making Good Preaching Better. Collegeville, Minnesota: The Liturgical Press.

Rummage, Stephen N. 2002. Planning Your Preaching. Grand Rapids, MI: Kregel.

Sakenfeld, Katherine D. 2008. The New Interpreter's Dictionary of the Bible. Nasville,TN: Abingdon Press.

The History of Gold Mining. 2017. http://youtu.be/sMKYSM7ydhk{accessed April 25, 2018}

Wardle, Terry. 1998. Draw Close to the Fire. Grand Rapids, MI: Chosen Books.

Wallace, Fisher E. 1979. Who Dares to preach? The Challenge of Biblical Preaching. Minneapolis, Minnesota: Augsburg Pub. House.

Wilson, Paul Scott. 2004. Broken Words. Nashville TN: Abingdon Press.

_____. 1992. A Concise History of Preaching. Nashville TN: Abingdon Press.

Printed in the United States
By Bookmasters